AMAZING ANIMALS OF THE WORLD ①

Volume 7

Owl, Pygmy — Robin, American

GROLIER
an imprint of

SCHOLASTIC
Scholastic Library Publishing
www.scholastic.com/librarypublishing

First published 2008 by Grolier, an imprint of Scholastic Inc.

© 2008 Scholastic Inc.

For information address the publisher: Grolier, Scholastic Library Publishing
90 Old Sherman Turnpike
Danbury, CT 06816

Printed and bound in the U.S.A.

Library of Congress Cataloging-in-Publication Data
Amazing animals of the world 1.
v. cm.
Contents: v. 1. Aardvark-bobcat — v. 2. Bobolink-cottonmouth — v. 3. Coyote-fish, Siamese fighting — v. 4. Fisher-hummingbird, ruby-throated — v. 5. Hyena, brown-mantis, praying — v. 6. Marmoset, common-owl, great horned — v. 7. Owl, pygmy-robin, American — v. 8. Sailfin, giant-spider, black widow — v. 9. Spider, garden-turtle, common musk — v. 10. Turtle, green sea-zebrafish.
Includes bibliographical references and index.
ISBN 0-7172-6225-1; 978-0-7172-6225-0 (set : alk. Paper) - ISBN 0-7172-6226-X; 978-0-7172-6226-7 (v. 1 : alk. paper) - ISBN 0-7172-6227-8; 978-0-7172-6227-4 (v. 2 : alk. paper) - ISBN 0-7172-6228-6; 978-0-7172-6228-1 (v. 3 : alk. paper) - ISBN 0-7172-6229-4; 978-7172-6229-8 (v. 4 : alk. paper) - ISBN 0-7172-6230-8; 978-7172-6230-4 (v. 5 : alk. paper) - ISBN 0-7172-6231-6; 978-0-7172-6231-1 (v. 6 : alk. paper) - ISBN 0-7172-6232-4; 978-0-7172-6232-8 (v. 7 : alk. paper) - ISBN 0-7172-6233-2; 978-0-7172-6233-5 (v. 8 : alk. paper) - ISBN 0-7172-6234-0; 978-0-7172-6234-2 (v. 9 : alk. paper) - ISBN 0-7172-6235-9; 978-0-7172-6235-9 (v. 10 : alk. paper)
1. Animals—Encyclopedias, Juvenile. I. Grolier Incorporated. II. Title: Amazing animals of the world one.
QL49.A453 2007
590.3—dc22
2007012982

About This Set

Amazing Animals of the World 1 brings you pictures of 400 exciting creatures, and important information about how and where they live.

Each page shows just one species, or individual type, of animal. They all fall into seven main categories, or groups, of animals (classes and phylums scientifically) identified on each page with an icon (picture)—amphibians, arthropods, birds, fish, mammals, other invertebrates, and reptiles. Short explanations of what these group names mean, and other terms used commonly in the set, appear in the Glossary.

Scientists use all kinds of groupings to help them sort out the thousands of types of animals that exist today and once wandered the earth (extinct species). *Kingdoms*, *classes*, *phylums*, *genus*, and *species* are among the key words here that are also explained in the Glossary.

Where animals live is important to know as well. Each of the species in this set lives in a particular place in the world, which you can see outlined on the map on each page. And in those places, the animals tend to favor a particular habitat—an environment the animal finds suitable for life—with food, shelter, and safety from predators that might eat it. There they also find ways to coexist with other animals in the area that might eat somewhat different food, use different homes, and so on.

Each of the main habitats is named on the page and given an icon, or picture, to help you envision it. The habitat names are further defined in the Glossary.

As well as being part of groups like species, animals fall into other categories that help us understand their lives or behavior. You will find these categories in the Glossary, where you will learn about carnivores, herbivores, and other types of animals.

And there is more information you might want about an animal—its size, diet, where it lives, and how it carries on its species—the way it creates its young. All these facts and more appear in the data boxes at the top of each page.

Finally, the set is arranged alphabetically by the most common name of the species. That puts most beetles, for example, together in a group so you can compare them easily.

But some animals' names are not so common, and they don't appear near others like them. For instance, the chamois is a kind of goat or antelope. To find animals that are similar—or to locate any species—look in the Index at the end of each book in the set. It lists all animals by their various names (you will find the Giant South American River Turtle under Turtle, Giant South American River, and also under its other name—Arrau). And you will find all birds, fish, and so on gathered under their broader groupings.

Similarly, smaller like groups appear in the Set Index as well—butterflies include swallowtails and blues, for example.

Table of Contents
Volume 7

Glossary..4

Owl, Pygmy..5

Owl, Screech..6

Owl, Snowy..7

Oyster, Eastern..8

Panda, Giant..9

Panda, Red...10

Pangolin, Cape...11

Parakeet, Monk..12

Parrot, Yellow-headed...13

Parrotfish, Queen..14

Parrotfish, Rainbow...15

Peafowl, Indian..16

Peeper, Spring...17

Penguin, Adelie..18

Penguin, Chinstrap..19

Penguin, King...20

Penguin, Little Blue...21

Penguin, Magellanic..22

Pheasant, Ring-Necked...23

Pig, Bearded..24

Pigeon, Passenger...25

Pintail...26

Platypus, Duck-billed...27

Porcupinefish...28

Puffin, Atlantic...29

Puma..30

Python, Ball..31

Quail, Common...32

Raccoon...33

Rattlesnake, Prairie...34

Rattlesnake, Timber...35

Rattlesnake, Western Diamondback....................................36

Raven, Common...37

Rhea, Darwin's...38

Rhinoceros, Black..39

Rhinoceros, Great Indian...40

Rhinoceros, Sumatran..41

Rhinoceros, White..42

Roadrunner, Greater..43

Robin, American...44

Set Index..45

Glossary

Amphibians—species usually born from eggs in water or wet places, which change (metamorphose) into land animals. Frogs and salamanders are typical. They breathe through their skin mainly and have no scales.

Arctic and Antarctic—icy, cold, dry areas at the ends of the globe that lack trees but are home to small plants that grow in thawed areas (tundra). Penguins and seals are common inhabitants.

Arthropods—animals with segmented bodies, hard outer skin, and jointed legs, such as spiders and crabs.

Birds—born from eggs, these creatures have wings and often can fly. Eagles, pigeons, and penguins are all birds, though penguins cannot fly through the air.

Carnivores—they are animals that eat other animals. Many species do eat each other sometimes, and a few eat dead animals. Lions kill their prey and eat it, while vultures clean up dead bodies of animals.

Cities, Towns, and Farms—places where people live and have built or used the land and share it with many species. Sometimes these animals live in human homes or just nearby.

Class—part, or division, of a phylum.

Deserts—dry, usually warm areas where animals often are more active on cooler nights or near water sources. Owls, scorpions, and jack rabbits are common in American deserts.

Endangered—some animals in this set are marked as endangered because it is possible they will become extinct soon.

Extinct—these species have died out completely for whatever reason.

Family—part of an order.

Fish—water animals (aquatic) that typically are born from eggs and breathe through gills. Trout and eels are fish, though whales and dolphins are not (they are mammals).

Forests and Mountains—places where evergreen (coniferous) and leaf-shedding (deciduous) trees are common, or that rise in elevation to make cool, separate habitats. Rain forests are different (see below).

Freshwater—lakes, rivers, and the like carry fresh water (unlike Oceans and Shores, where the water is salty). Fish and birds abound, as do insects, frogs, and mammals.

Genus—part of a family.

Grasslands—habitats with few trees and light rainfall. Grasslands often lie between forests and deserts, and they are home to birds, coyotes, antelope, and snakes, as well as many other kinds of animals.

Herbivores—these animals eat mainly plants. Typical are hoofed animals (ungulates) that are common on grasslands, such as antelope or deer. Domestic (nonwild) ones are cows and horses.

Hibernators—species that live in harsh areas with very cold winters slow down their functions then become inactive or dormant.

Invertebrates—animals that lack backbones or internal skeletons. Many, such as insects and shrimp, have hard outer coverings. Clams and worms are also invertebrates.

Kingdom—the largest division of species. All living things are classified in one of the five kingdoms: animals, plants, fungi, protists, and monerans.

Mammals—these creatures usually bear live young and feed them on milk from the mother. A few lay eggs (monotremes like the platypus) or nurse young in a pouch (marsupials like opossums and kangaroos).

Migrators—some species spend different seasons in different places, moving to where more food, warmth, or safety can be found. Birds often do this, sometimes over long distances, but other types of animals also move seasonally, including fish and mammals.

Oceans and Shores—seawater is salty, often deep, and huge. In it live many fish, invertebrates, and some mammals, such as whales and dolphins. On the shore, birds and other creatures often gather.

Order—part of a class.

Phylum—part of a kingdom.

Rain forests—here huge trees grow among many other plants helped by the warm, wet environment. Thousands of species of animals also live in these rich habitats.

Reptiles—these species have scales, have lungs to breathe, and lay eggs or give birth to live young. Dinosaurs are thought to have been reptiles, while today the class includes turtles, snakes, lizards, and crocodiles.

Scientific Name—the genus and species name of a creature in Latin. For instance, *Canis lupus* is the wolf. Scientific names avoid the confusion possible with common names in any one language or across languages.

Species—a group of the same type of living thing. Part of an order.

Subspecies—a variety but quite similar part of a species.

Territorial—many animals mark out and defend a patch of ground as their home area. Birds and mammals may call very small or very large spots their territories.

Vertebrates—animals with backbones and skeletons under their skins.

Pygmy Owl
Glaucidium passerinum

Length: 6¼ inches
Weight: 2½ ounces (female); 2 ounces (male)
Diet: mice, shrews, and small birds
Number of Eggs: usually 5 to 7

Home: Europe and Central Asia
Order: goatsuckers, owls
Family: typical owls

Forests and Mountains

Birds

© FRANCESC MUNTADA / CORBIS

For such a small bird, the pygmy owl is a surprisingly fierce hunter. Its large eyes have thickened corneas that act as magnifying glasses. These help the owl spot mice and other prey. The owl also has excellent hearing. This is owed to a large ear opening on each side of its head. Upon hearing even the slightest sound of a little animal as it walks along a branch or on the forest floor, the owl will swoop down and grab the prey with its sharp, curved claws. It carries the prey up to a high tree branch. There the owl enjoys a leisurely meal. Pygmy owls store extra food in caves and other places much the way squirrels hide nuts for the winter. They use this food when they cannot find enough fresh food.

The presence of pygmy owls in a tree is usually indicated by piles of waste pellets at the foot of the tree. Another way to learn if pygmy owls are nearby is to listen to songbirds. Songbirds know that the owls are their enemies. When songbirds see a pygmy owl or hear it sing, they join together to mob the owl. The group of songbirds noisily attacks the owl. Then they try to kill it or chase it away.

Pygmy owls form lifelong pairs, mating each year in spring. The eggs are laid in tree holes made by woodpeckers and are incubated by the female. She leaves the eggs briefly when the male calls, telling her that he has brought her food. Both parents raise the young owlets. They first leave the nest when they are about four weeks old.

Screech Owl
Megascops asio

Length: 7 to 10 inches
Wingspan: 18 to 24 inches
Weight: 3 to 7¾ ounces
(females); 3 to 6 ounces
(males)
Diet: mostly mice, shrews, and
insects

Number of Eggs: 3 to 8
Home: North America
Order: goatsuckers, owls
Family: typical owls

Cities, Towns,
and Farms

Birds

© JOE MCDONALD / CORBIS

The little screech owl is unfairly named. It does not screech. Rather, its most common call resembles a soft, trembling cry. In some places, this bird is called the shivering owl. Its "shivering" cry gives superstitious people the shivers, too. Still other people call it the long-eared owl. This name came from the large tufts of feathers that make the bird's ears look bigger than they actually are. The owl raises or lowers its ear tufts as a means of communicating with its fellow owls. For example, when a screech owl lowers its ear tufts, it may be telling another owl that it is about to attack.

Screech owls hunt soon after sunset. They fly over woods, fields, and lakeshores in search of prey. They eat many insect pests, such as grasshoppers, locusts, and beetles, as well as large numbers of mice. Their eating habits make owls very helpful to farmers and other people. For this reason they should be carefully protected.

Screech owls either nest in hollow trees or take over nests deserted by other birds. They will also build nests in special boxes placed in trees for their use. The female screech owl sits on the eggs until they hatch. Her mate usually brings her food during this time. Both parents provide food for the newly hatched owlets. The parents are very protective of the owlets. They may dive at or even hit people who wander too close to the nest.

Snowy Owl
Bubo scandiacus

Length: 20 to 24 inches
Weight: 1.6–6.5 pounds
Wingspan: 4½ feet
Diet: rodents, rabbits, and birds

Number of Eggs: 7 to 15
Home: northern Canada, Europe, and Asia
Order: goatsuckers, owls
Family: typical owls

  Arctic and Antarctic

Birds

© STEVE KAUFMAN / CORBIS

The snowy owl's white color helps the bird blend in with its home in the tundra—vast, cold plains along the northern rim of North America, Europe, and Asia. The Arctic tundra is an unusual place, and there the snowy owl has to live a much different life from most other owls. Most owls live in trees. There are no trees on the tundra, so the snowy owl must nest on the ground. Most owls hunt at night. The sun never sets during the Arctic summer, so snowy owls must hunt in the brightness of a 24-hour day.

The tundra is also home to millions of hamsterlike animals called lemmings, the snowy owl's favorite meal. The lemming population tends to rise steadily for a few years. At their peak, these little animals can be seen scurrying everywhere. Their numbers then rapidly decline for a year or two. This population cycle has a great effect on snowy owls. The owls have chicks only during years when lemmings are abundant. When the lemmings are scarce, the owls cannot afford to be confined to a nest. During these lean times, they must travel far outside their normal range to search for ducks, sea gulls, and other prey.

Snowy owls also fly south in the winter—but not too far. In North America, they usually remain in Canada and the most-northern parts of the United States. They can sometimes be seen even farther south during years when lemmings are scarce.

Eastern Oyster
Crassostrea virginica

Length: up to 10 inches
Width: up to 4 inches
Diet: plant and animal matter
Number of Eggs: 10 million to 20 million

Home: Gulf and Atlantic coasts of North America
Order: oysters and relatives
Family: oysters

 Oceans and Shores

 Other Invertebrates

© GILBERT S. GRANT / PHOTO RESEARCHERS

Eastern oysters are a delicious and popular seafood. They are enjoyed not only by humans but also by birds, fish, crabs, and many other animals. The starfish consumes eastern oysters in a unique way. First, it pulls open the oyster's shell. Then the starfish turns its stomach inside out through its mouth and puts its stomach inside the oyster. Chemicals produced by the starfish's stomach digest the soft parts of the oyster—within its own shell!

The eastern oyster has a thick, heavy shell made of two parts, called valves. These are connected by a hinge. The lower valve is larger than the upper valve. The oyster is permanently attached by the lower valve to a hard object in the water. Eastern oysters live in the shallow, brackish water normally found in bays and near the mouths of rivers. These are areas where fresh water enters and mixes with the ocean.

Eastern oysters produce enormous numbers of eggs. A single female may produce 100 million eggs a year! The eggs are microscopic. Five hundred of them in a line will equal only 1 inch. Fertilization takes place in the sea. A few days later, the eggs hatch into larvae that swim about for a day or two. Then they change their shape and settle down onto a hard object. Most eggs and larvae do not survive. Many are washed ashore or out to sea. Many more are eaten by other animals.

Giant Panda
Ailuropoda melanoleuca

Length: 6 feet
Height: up to 5 feet
Weight: up to 330 pounds
Diet: bamboo

Number of Young: 1
Home: west-central China
Order: carnivores
Family: bears

 Forests and Mountains

 Mammals

 Endangered Animals

© KEREN SU / CORBIS

The giant panda lives in bamboo forests in west-central China. In summer it stays mainly on high plateaus. During the winter it moves to the valleys. Pandas were first discovered by western nations in 1869. They began appearing in zoos outside China in the late 1930s. And they have been popular animals ever since. They are very rare. There may be fewer than 1,000 left. Farming and forest development destroy their natural surroundings.

Giant pandas look like teddy bears. But scientists at one time classified them in the raccoon family. Today, scientists agree that the giant panda is a special kind of bear. The giant panda weighs more than 200 pounds. Its favorite food is bamboo. It chews it with its powerful teeth. Females give birth to a single cub in August or September. The mother lovingly cares for the cub. Young pandas are very active and playful. It is rare for a panda to give birth in a zoo. When this happens, newspapers write about it.

In the wild, pandas eat bamboo shoots. They eat more than 80 pounds of bamboo a day. Pandas in zoos sometimes eat meat. A panda sits down to eat. This frees its forepaws, which it uses like claws. The paws have six fingers. One of them is a special thumb. The thumb helps pandas hold plant stems. Pandas are always hungry. A panda spends 16 out of every 24 hours eating!

Red Panda
Ailurus fulgens

Length: 20 to 25 inches
Length of Tail: 40 to 45 inches
Weight: 6½ to 11 pounds
Diet: acorns, roots, lichens, bamboo shoots; some insects

Number of Young: 1 to 4
Home: southern Central Asia
Order: carnivores
Family: bears

 Forests and Mountains

Mammals

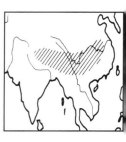

? Endangered Animals

© RON AUSTING / FRANK LANE PICTURE AGENCY / CORBIS

The giant panda is among the most famous and popular animals, but the red panda is hardly known by most people. It does not look like the giant panda at all. It looks more like a fox, with its beautiful red coat, long fluffy tail, and pointed snout. The Chinese call it *hyn-ho*, which means "fox of fire." Red pandas puzzled Europeans when they first found them, but Americans thought they were a kind of raccoon. Because of this, the giant panda, really a bear, was also once classed as a strange raccoon. Today it is known that the two "pandas" are not closely related.

The red panda eats mostly plants, especially bamboo shoots. It is usually active at night or early in the morning. Days are for sleeping. Curled up, it sleeps in trees or balances on branches. Red pandas are good climbers and can jump more than 5 feet between branches. But they are clumsy on the ground and move slowly with an odd, pigeon-toed waddle.

Red pandas make small, sharp whistling sounds like those of birds. If they are attacked, they stand up, growl, and spit, a little like cats do when they are trapped. They are by nature very peaceful and rather playful. But their razorlike claws and sharp teeth prevent them from being good pets. Red pandas live among bamboo forests very near the Himalaya mountain chain. There are very few red pandas in the world, and like giant pandas, they are endangered.

Cape Pangolin
Manis temminckii

Length of Body: 20 inches
Length of Tail: 14 inches
Weight: about 2 pounds
Diet: termites and ants
Number of Young: 1

Home: tropical and subtropical Africa
Order: pangolins, scaly anteaters
Family: pangolins

 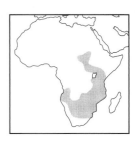
Grasslands

Mammals

© NIGEL DENNIS / PHOTO RESEARCHERS

Endangered Animals

At first glance, a cape pangolin looks like a big lizard. The tops of its head, body, and tail are covered with large scales that overlap like roof shingles. Pangolins are the only mammals that have this kind of covering. The pangolin gets its name from a Malayan word, pĕngguling. This means "round cushion." It is an appropriate description. The pangolin rolls up into a round ball to sleep and to protect itself from enemies.

The cape pangolin is a ground dweller. It rests during the day in burrows and searches for food at night. It does not have very good eyesight or hearing. It must therefore depend on its sense of smell to find termite or ant nests. When it sniffs out such a structure, the pangolin tears open the nest with its strong claws. Then it uses its long, sticky tongue to lick up the inhabitants. A pangolin rarely destroys an entire insect nest. Enough of the nest usually survives so that the insects can rebuild. This helps ensure a continuing source of food for the pangolin. While it eats, the pangolin closes its eyes, ears, and nostrils to protect itself from insect bites.

At birth a baby cape pangolin weighs less than 1 pound. At first its scales are soft and not overlapping. But they become hard within a few days. When its mother travels in search of food, the baby perches on her back. It sits above the base of the tail and goes along for the ride!

Monk Parakeet
Myiopsitta monachus

Length: about 11½ inches
Weight: about 3½ ounces
Diet: seeds, fruits, berries, nuts, blossoms, leaves, insects, and grubs
Number of Eggs: 5 to 8

Home: native to South America; introduced to North America and Puerto Rico
Order: parrots and relatives
Family: cockatoos, lories

 Cities, Towns, and Farms

 Birds

© LAWRENCE NAYLOR / PHOTO RESEARCHERS

The monk parakeet is a popular cage bird. It comes from Brazil, Argentina, and Bolivia. Like many parakeets, monks occasionally escape. Most cage birds do not live long in the wild. But the monk parakeet is a hearty bird. It is able to survive in North America. Monk parakeets do not go far into the wilderness. This medium-sized parrot has taken a liking to North American cities. Some of the largest colonies are in New York and Chicago. They have as many as 200 parakeets.

Monk parakeets weave large stick nests. They build their nests in treetops. Their colonies look like enormous wicker baskets. A community nest has up to 20 "apartments." Each one is occupied by a mated pair. The large nest provides a warm shelter for the birds. It helps them to survive the cold winter. Most of the birds die if people remove the nests.

Monk parakeets are colorful birds. Many people are thrilled to have them in their neighborhood. But the monk parakeet is a noisy neighbor. It shrieks constantly. And it has a loud warning call. Monk parakeets are agricultural pests. In South America, this bird causes great damage to crops.

Yellow-headed Parrot
Amazona ochrocephala

Length: up to 15 inches
Diet: fruits and seeds
Number of Eggs: 1 to 3

Home: South America
Order: parrots and relatives
Family: cockatoos, lories

 Rain Forests

 Birds

The yellow-headed parrot is one of 26 species of parrots called blunt-tails. Like most of its cousins, the yellow-headed parrot has a green body and a colorful face. This particular species has a bright yellow forehead, from which it gets its name. It can also be recognized by its red wing joints.

The yellow-headed parrot lives in the jungle canopy among a tangle of leaves, vines, and branches. In such a crowded environment, it spends more time climbing than flying. In fact, blunt-tailed parrots are awkward flyers. Many don't seem to mind living in captivity, where they can't fly at all. The yellow-headed parrot is very skilled at using its feet as hands. Sailors—who have long kept these parrots as pets—say the birds can even unlatch hooks and untie knots to make mischief in cabinets and storage bins.

The yellow-headed parrot is also dexterous with its large beak, which it uses like a third hand. This "hand," however, is powerful enough to crack the shells of most any kind of nut. Parrots also hang and swing from their beaks as they climb among the treetops in their jungle homes. Another unique feature of a parrot's body is its toes. Rather than pointing in the same direction, two of the parrot's toes curl backward, while the other two bend forward. This arrangement makes the parrot's foot a powerful yet delicate clamp for grasping branches and holding food.

Queen Parrotfish
Scarus vetula

Length: up to 24 inches
Diet: coral and algae
Method of Reproduction: egg layer

Home: coral reefs from Bermuda south to Colombia
Order: perch-like fishes
Family: parrotfishes

Oceans and Shores

Fish

© HAL BERAL / CORBIS

Queen parrotfish live among coral reefs in warm, shallow waters. They are native to Bermuda, Florida, the Bahamas, and the West Indies. They're often seen in small groups consisting of several females and one male.

Queen parrotfish are easy to recognize. The teeth in their jaws grow together to form a structure that looks like a parrot's beak. Parrotfish feed during the daytime. They use their powerful beak to scrape off material from the reefs. Teeth in their throat allow them to grind this material. They digest the algae and coral animals. But they excrete the indigestible rocklike coral that has protected these tiny organisms. Such eating habits help the coral-reef community by wearing down reefs and producing sand. At night the queen parrotfish settles to the bottom of the sea. It makes its own sleeping bag by secreting a jellylike cocoon of mucus around itself. This helps to protect the resting parrotfish against moray eels and other predators.

The queen parrotfish has an unusual life cycle. It features a variety of colors and sexual phases. The organs for both sexes are present. But they appear at different times in the fish's life. All young parrotfish are dull-colored females with a white stripe along each side. As the fish grow older, they turn into brightly colored green blue males with touches of orange along the edges of the scales.

Rainbow Parrotfish
Scarus guacamaia

Length: up to 37½ inches
Diet: algae and sea grasses
Method of Reproduction: egg layer
Home: Gulf of Mexico and eastern Atlantic Ocean from Bermuda to Argentina

Order: perch-like fishes
Family: parrotfishes

 Oceans and Shores

 Fish

© TOM ZURAW / ANIMALS ANIMALS / EARTHSCENES

The parrotfish is named for its parrotlike "beak," which is actually made up of teeth that have fused together. This bluish green beak is perfectly designed for scraping algae off coral reefs and for grazing on sea grass. Inside the parrotfish's mouth is a second set of teeth. The fish uses these inner molars for grinding soft rocks and dead coral shells into sand. The fish does not actually digest the sand. Instead, it removes the nutritious algae locked between the grains.

Parrotfish are often the most abundant fish around a coral reef. Both sexes look very similar. When young, they are brown on top and pale below, with two stripes along each side. As they mature, the rainbows become more colorful. The young adults may be reddish, turning a bright green in later life.

Each rainbow parrotfish makes its home in a small cave, where it retires at night. It also uses its private cave to flee when danger is near. In coastal estuaries, parrotfish hide among the roots of mangrove trees as well.

Rainbow parrotfish are important food fish for the people of the Caribbean. Typically they are caught in traps or by spearing and are sold fresh in local markets. More recently parrotfish have appeared in stores in the eastern United States. These fish are usually imported from Jamaica or Antigua and marketed in large fish bazaars, such as the Fulton Fish Market in New York City.

Indian Peafowl
Pavo cristatus

Length: 7½ feet (male)
Diet: seeds, shoots of plants, insects, and small animals
Number of Eggs: 8 to 20
Home: India, Sri Lanka, Bangladesh

Order: pheasants, quails, and relatives
Family: grouse, partridges

 Forests and Mountains

 Birds

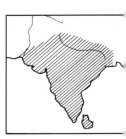

© TERRY W. EGGERS / CORBIS

In the past, peafowl lived on castle grounds. Now they can be seen in many parks and gardens. Peafowl originally came from India. They still live there in the wild. The peafowl has been domesticated for more than 2,000 years.

Only the peacock, or the male, has the immense fan tail. It is almost 5 feet wide. He spreads his tail out to impress the peahen, or the female. When he opens it, thousands of colorful "eyes" appear. At this time the peacock is "in its pride." When the peacock shows his beautiful feathers, he also makes them vibrate with soft gentle sounds. From the front, the peacock's bright blue body looks like a jewel in a box made of colorful feathers.

The peafowl is a giant pheasant. The Indian peafowl lives in the tropical forest. It has long, strong legs. It eats plants, grasses, or grains. It also eats insects, mollusks, and small animals. It is a sociable animal. Every evening, the peafowl perches on a branch. Its loud, metallic voice is heard well into the night.

The peahen has more subdued colors. She is almost invisible when she covers her eggs. Her colors look like patches of light on the surrounding bushes. She lays between 8 and 20 eggs. She sits alone on her nest.

Spring Peeper
Pseudacris crucifer

Length: ¾ to 1¼ inches
Diet: insects
Method of Reproduction: egg layer

Home: eastern North America
Order: frogs and toads
Family: New World tree frogs

  Forests and Mountains

Amphibians

It is evening in the early spring. A small brownish frog comes out from under a pile of leaves. It looks around with its tiny, bulging eyes. Suddenly a high, shrill whistling sound comes out of its mouth. Soon it is joined by other little brown frogs. Their chorus of musical croaks begins to sound like the jingling of sleigh bells. These are spring peepers. They have just come out of winter hibernation. They are announcing the arrival of spring. Their loud peeping can be heard almost a mile away.

The spring peeper is one of the most common frogs in North America. It lives in the eastern half of the United States and southeastern Canada. Its scientific name is

Pseudacris crucifer, or *hyla crucifer*. It lives in wooded areas or near flooded ponds and swamps.

The spring peeper is considered a tree frog. But it actually climbs only small bushes. It comes out of the bushes to hibernate or mate. After mating, the female lays her eggs in a nearby marsh, swamp, pond, or pool. The eggs hatch in two or three weeks. As with other frogs, the spring peeper young go through a larval stage; that is, they are tadpoles that live in the water. This larval stage lasts for about three months. After that spring peepers begin their life on land.

Adelie Penguin
Pygoscelis adeliae

Length: 30 inches
Weight: 9 to 14 pounds
Diet: fish and invertebrates
Number of Eggs: 2
Home: Antarctica and surrounding islands

Order: auks, herons, and relatives
Family: penguins

Arctic and Antarctic

Birds

© PAUL A. SOUDERS / CORBIS

Adelie penguins live in colonies of up to 300,000 birds. These colonies, called rookeries, are densely packed. From a distance, the penguins look more like plants than animals. Adelie penguins are sociable. This means that they get along well with others. But they are also territorial. This means that they protect their own turf. Each penguin couple lives on its own patch of ground. This patch may be smaller than a square yard. But the pair defends it fiercely from fellow penguins and other animals.

Adelie penguins usually mate for life. They choose their mates in October. This is springtime in the Southern Hemisphere. Males and females go their separate ways in the winter. The next spring, the penguins return to the site of their old nest. Then a couple must find each other again. How do you think they do this? They recognize each other by voice.

Both male and female Adelie penguins gather stones for a nest. The female usually lays her eggs in November. The eggs hatch a month later. Both parents feed and protect the chicks. The mother and father penguins change places frequently. One guards the chicks while the other gets food. The parents greet each other noisily when they switch. Thousands of penguin couples live in a colony. Therefore, this coming and going makes a loud, continuous racket.

Chinstrap Penguin
Pygoscelis antarctica

Length: 20 inches
Weight: 8 pounds
Diet: krill, squid, and fish
Number of Eggs: 2

Home: Antarctic coast
Order: auks, herons, and relatives
Family: penguins

 Arctic and Antarctic

 Birds

© KEVIN SCHAFER / CORBIS

At first glance a sailor might mistake a flock of chinstrap penguins for a school of small dolphins. These flightless birds speed through the waters off Antarctica in large hunting parties. They skim the surface at speeds of up to 20 miles per hour, dipping and jumping together in a behavior called "porpoising." This allows the penguins to come up for air without slowing their swimming speed. Their tongues and mouths are lined with sharp, backward-pointing spines, which enable the birds to quickly and firmly grab onto slippery squid and krill—again without ever slowing down!

The chinstrap penguin looks like it is wearing a black swimming cap tied neatly beneath its chin. Like all penguins, the members of this species propel themselves through the water with strong, paddlelike wings. Their large breastbone is shaped like the keel of a ship, helping them to easily cut through the water. The rest of the penguin's body is compact and streamlined. It drags its short legs behind like a rudder, using its webbed feet to steer and brake.

Because the chinstrap penguin lives in Antarctica, it seldom has fresh water to drink. Instead, it eats huge amounts of snow. Penguins also have special glands above their eyes that enable them to secrete salt from their bodies. This allows them to drink a limited amount of seawater without harming their bodies.

King Penguin
Aptenodytes patagonicus

Height: 35 to 37 inches
Diet: squid, shellfish, and fish
Number of Eggs: 1
Home: various Antarctic islands

Order: auks, herons, and relatives
Family: penguins

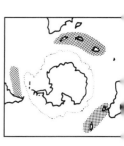

Arctic and Antarctic

Birds

© TIM DAVIS / CORBIS

People sometimes confuse penguins with auks. However, it is easy to tell them apart. Penguins cannot fly, whereas auks, except for the now-extinct great auk, can. Also, penguins live in the Southern Hemisphere and auks in the Northern Hemisphere.

Penguins are popular at zoos, and the king penguin is the most popular penguin of all. Very large, standing upright on its short legs, it waddles when it walks. Its head is slender, and it has a long pointed beak.

The king penguin breeds on islands in the south Atlantic and Indian Oceans, such as the Falkland Islands and South Georgia. From October to April, thousands of birds go to these remote islands to mate. They lay eggs in two periods: November-December and February-March. The female lays one egg on the ground. Then she rolls it onto her feet with the help of her beak and puts it in a fold of her skin to keep it warm. Both male and female take care of the egg, literally "standing" turns for 5-day shifts. Eggs hatch after 55 days. Until they are one month old, the little birds stay near their parents. After that, they are gathered together, and a few adults watch over this "day-care center" while others feed at sea. The king penguin is well adapted to marine life. Its wings act as both oars and fins. King penguins swim at great speed. They can dive very deep to catch their prey—squid, shellfish, and fish.

Little Blue Penguin
Eudyptula minor

Height: 15 inches
Weight: 3 pounds
Diet: fish and squid
Number of Eggs: 2
Home: New Zealand, Tasmania, and southern Australia

Order: auks, herons, and relatives
Family: penguins

Oceans and Shores

Birds

© TOM BRAKEFIELD / CORBIS

The little blue, also called the fairy, is the world's smallest penguin. Penguins as a whole tend to be bold and noisy birds. But the little blue of the family is shy and timid. It lives on remote beaches and islands in and around southern Australia and New Zealand. The little blue is quick to flee from humans. But sailors passing in the night often hear the bird's sad cry. Its call has been compared to the mewing of a stranded cat.

Little blue penguins mate for life. Yet couples spend much of the year apart. At the beginning of breeding season, the male and female return to the previous year's nest site. There they greet each other with a brief courtship dance.

The female little blue lays her eggs in an underground burrow or in a deep rock crevice. Both parents take turns warming the eggs. Whenever one parent is relieved of its duty, it immediately dives into the ocean to hunt for food. Like all penguins, little blues also share in rearing their young. Until the chicks are old enough to swim, they are fed regurgitated fish from their parents' stomachs.

The little blue penguin never ventures too far into the frigid southern seas. It prefers to hunt for fish in shallow water. Although it is not as plump as other penguins, the little blue has a thick layer of fat to help keep it warm. Its feathers are short and stiff and form a waterproof coat.

Magellanic Penguin
Spheniscus magellanicus

Length: 25 inches
Weight: 10 pounds
Diet: small fish
Number of Eggs: 2

Home: Chile and Argentina
Order: auks, herons, and relatives
Family: penguins

Oceans and Shores

Birds

© KEREN SU / CORBIS

Magellanic penguins are large, flightless birds. They nest by the millions under bushes and around rocks near the Strait of Magellan. Their colonies on these South American beaches date back thousands of years.

Magellanic penguins are monogamous. This means they have one mate for life. Both males and females help tend nests, warm eggs, and feed the young. The females lay their eggs in October. This is spring in the Southern Hemisphere. The birds escape the cold of the winter by moving north for several months. Like all penguins, this species does not fly. They walk with a peculiar waddle, wagging their heads from side to side as they move. Penguins need to turn their heads constantly because their eyes are on the sides of their head, not the front. To tell how far away an object is, the penguin must look at it first with one eye and then the other. Humans have an easier time judging distances. That is because they can look at something with both eyes at the same time.

Penguins are slow and clumsy on land. But they are speedy and graceful underwater. They use their short wings as fins as they zoom around like agile submarines. Penguins can remain underwater for two minutes before coming up for air. While in the water, they must be careful to avoid sea lions. The sea lions' appetite for penguins make them the birds' most fearsome enemy.

Ring-Necked Pheasant
Phasianus colchicus

Length: 2½ to 3 feet
Weight: 1.3–4.4 pounds
Diet: seeds, berries, and other vegetation
Number of Eggs: 6 to 15

Home: Eurasia and North America
Order: pheasants, quails, and relatives
Family: grouse, partridges

 Grasslands

 Birds

© D. ROBERT & LORRI FRANZ / CORBIS

The ring-necked pheasant is a popular game bird. It is hunted in many parts of the United States. This large chickenlike bird originated in China. It was introduced into Europe and then into the United States in the 1800s. In China it lived on the forested slopes of mountains. But in the United States it lives mainly on grasslands and farmlands. It is most common on the central plains in the northern part of the country.

Both the male and the female ring-necked pheasant have short, stocky wings. They cannot fly great distances. But they have strong legs and feet and are very quick on the ground. They use their speed to escape from enemies. The hen weighs about 10 pounds less than the cock. She uses her colors to hide from enemies. Her dark and light brown feathers blend in with bushes and other vegetation. The male ring-necked pheasant is much more colorful than the female. Brilliant green head feathers surround a red eye patch of bare skin. The white ring around its neck gives the bird its name. The feathers on the body and the long, narrow tail are shades of brown.

Ring-necked pheasants are most common in fields, pastures, and farmlands. The females build their nests on the ground or in a hollow. There they are hidden by grass, weeds, or shrubbery. The brownish eggs hatch in about three and a half weeks. The chicks are ready to fly one week after they hatch.

Bearded Pig
Sus barbatus

Length: 5 feet
Weight: 350 to 400 pounds
Diet: fruits, roots, and insect larvae
Number of Young: 2 to 8

Home: Southeast Asia
Order: even-toed hoofed mammals
Family: pigs and hogs

 Rain Forests

 Mammals

The bearded pig is not one of nature's beauties. A ragged beard hangs from its cheeks. Large, bristly warts grow between and under its eyes. The pig's beauty comes from the way it has learned to cooperate with other animals. It allows crowned wood partridges to ride on its back. The partridge picks ticks from the pig's skin. Bearded pigs also follow troops of gibbons and macaques swinging through the trees. The lucky pigs dine on the fruit that the primates accidentally drop to the ground.

Bearded pigs usually find all the food they need on the floor of the tropical forest. But sometimes they raid the fields of local villages. They can do great damage rooting up yam fields and other crops. Most of the people in Borneo and Sumatra are Muslim. So the pigs have little to fear. The Muslim religion forbids eating pork. The animals' only other predator is the clouded leopard.

Each year, the bearded pigs in northern Borneo migrate to the southern part of the island. Their urge to migrate is powerful. They will hardly stop to eat or rest until their journey is done.

Like humans, bearded pigs have no specific mating season. But generally they have babies just once a year. The pregnant female leaves her herd to build a huge nest. It is 3 feet high and made of palm branches and other vegetation. The piglets stay with their mother for about a year.

Passenger Pigeon
Ectopistes migratorius

Length: 17 inches
Diet: nuts, berries, seeds, and worms
Number of Eggs: 1 or 2
Home: eastern United States and southern Canada

Date of Extinction: 1914
Order: doves, pigeons
Family: doves, pigeons

 Forests and Mountains

Birds

 Extinct Animals

© PHOTO RESEARCHERS

At one time, billions of passenger pigeons could be seen migrating together. They flew 60 miles per hour, in flocks a mile wide and 240 miles long. Observers wrote that these gigantic migratory groups nearly darkened the sky. Needless to say, these enormous flocks caused a lot of damage. The pigeons ate every scrap of suitable food in an area. They broke off countless tree branches. They even toppled trees with their combined weight.

Scientists suspect that passenger pigeons formed the huge flocks as a defense against predators. Individual passenger pigeons were almost defenseless. But for a long time, there were never enough predators in one place to sufficiently reduce the flock as

a whole. Then came human hunters. American Indians hunted passenger pigeons for food for centuries. European settlers began overhunting passenger pigeons in the 1600s and 1700s. But the really bad news came in the middle of the 1800s. At this time people started hunting these birds in large organized groups. Thousands of professional pigeon hunters followed the flocks from state to state. They netted the birds and stuffed them into barrels, 500 at a time. By 1896 the birds were scarce, and the netters were out of work. Laws were passed to protect the pigeons. Sadly, however, the population of passenger pigeons never recovered. The last passenger pigeon died in a Cincinnati zoo in 1914.

Pintail
Anas acuta

Length: 25 to 29 inches (male); 21 to 23 inches (female)
Diet: mainly seeds of aquatic plants
Number of Eggs: 6 to 12
Home: North America, Central America, Europe, Asia, and Africa

Order: ducks, geese, swans, waterfowl
Family: ducks, geese, and swans

 Freshwater

 Birds

© DARRELL GULIN / CORBIS

Pintails are the only freshwater ducks in North America with a long, pointed tail. A pair of pintails makes a beautiful sight. The two birds are very different in appearance. Male pintails are larger and heavier than females. They have a dark brown head, a white neck, a gray back, and white underparts. The female pintail has speckled brown feathers.

Pintails migrate northward to breed in early spring. They are graceful fliers. Their long, narrow wings allow them to soar with little wind resistance. Pintails make their nests on the ground, usually in tall grasses near ponds. The female lines the nest with her own soft down feathers. She incubates her eggs for about three weeks before they

hatch. The ducklings require constant care. They are not ready to fly until they are about six weeks old.

In autumn, pintails leave their northern breeding grounds and fly to warmer climates. This is a dangerous time for the pintails. Hunters shoot and kill many of these migrating birds. Other pintails die after flying into obstacles such as telephone and electrical wires. Pintails that fly 2,000 miles across the Pacific Ocean to winter in Hawaii may lose their way and die. Those that survive the fall migration gather in large groups in their wintering places. One wildlife refuge near Sacramento, California, is the winter home to more than 1 million pintails!

Duck-billed Platypus
Ornithorhynchus anatinus

Length: 16 to 22 inches
Weight: 1½ to 5 pounds
Diet: worms, crustaceans, fish, and other small aquatic animals

Number of Eggs: usually 2
Home: eastern Australia and Tasmania
Order: monotremes
Family: platypus

  Freshwater

Mammals

© TOM MCHUGH / PHOTO RESEARCHERS

The duck-billed platypus is different from other animals. In fact, when scientists first heard it, many refused to believe it existed. The platypus is a mammal. It has fur and milk-producing glands. But its snout looks like a duck's bill. And it lays eggs that look like reptile eggs. The flat snout is covered with skin that contains many nerve endings. The platypus hunts along the bottom of the river. It uses its snout to feel for food. Crayfish, shrimp, worms, and other small animals are its prey. It eats most of the food it finds right away. It may store some food in its cheek pouches. It eats that later. The adult platypus does not have teeth. So how does it eat? It uses its snout to pick up sand and gravel. The snout also grinds the food.

The platypus is an excellent swimmer. It uses its webbed feet to swim and its broad, flat tail to guide itself through the water. Male platypuses can kill small animals. They can also cause painful wounds in larger animals. They do this with the help of a poison spur on each back foot. And where does the platypus go when it's not in the water? It heads for a den that it has dug in the riverbank. Platypuses come together only to mate. Before they do, the female digs a new, deeper den. She lines it with grass. Then she lays the eggs. The female stays with the eggs until the chicks hatch. After birth, the young platypuses cling to the hair on their mother's stomach. They lick up milk that oozes through her skin.

Porcupinefish
Diodon hystrix

Length: up to 3 feet
Width: up to 3 feet when inflated
Weight: 5 to 10 pounds
Diet: crustaceans and mollusks

Home: Atlantic Ocean, Pacific Ocean, Gulf of Mexico, and the Caribbean
Order: cowfishes, filefishes
Family: burrfishes

 Oceans and Shores

 Fish

© HAL BERAL / CORBIS

You can easily guess from its name that this fish is covered with long quills. Most of the time, the porcupinefish's quills lie flat against its body. But when the fish is scared or angered, it inflates like a balloon. This makes the spines spring straight out in a threatening way. This frightening sight is enough to scare away most predators.

Humans, on the other hand, find the sight of a puffed-up porcupinefish both amusing and fascinating. Dried porcupinefish are popular items in seaside souvenir shops. The specimens that are sold as souvenirs are typically about the size of a spine-covered basketball. But in the wild, porcupinefish can grow three times as large.

The porcupinefish seldom ventures far from shore and only rarely into water deeper than 50 or 60 feet. Snorkelers who frequent these areas will tell you that the creature is quite shy and will not let them approach too closely. But porcupinefish can be tamed. Those kept in saltwater aquariums can be taught to take food from their owner's hand.

The jaws of the porcupinefish are fused together to form a hard beak. It looks much like a tortoise's jaw. It has only two teeth in its unusual mouth. It uses them to crack open the shells of crustaceans and mollusks, which it never tires of eating.

Atlantic Puffin
Fratercula arctica

Length: 12 to 13 inches
Wingspan: 21 to 24 inches
Diet: mainly fish
Number of Eggs: 1
Home: coastal areas of the North Atlantic and the Arctic Ocean

Order: auks, herons, and relatives
Family: gulls, puffins, terns, and relatives

Oceans and Shores

Birds

© KEVIN SCHAFER / CORBIS

When sailors at sea spot a few Atlantic puffins, they know they are close to land. Puffins live in the North Atlantic and Arctic Oceans. They are found along seacoasts and on islands. They nest in large colonies. These colonies often include auks, gulls, and other birds. There the Atlantic puffin—usually the male—builds a nest. The female lays one white egg in it. The parents stay together through the nesting season. They both care for the young.

Puffins are also called sea parrots. They get this nickname because of their large beak. It is shaped like a triangle. During the mating season, this beak develops an outer covering. Its red, blue, and yellow colors are brilliant. The covering, or sheath, falls off after the mating season. It leaves behind a less colorful, yellow-tipped beak. Atlantic puffins are excellent divers and swimmers. They fly overhead or swim on the surface of the water until they spot prey. Then they dive. They quickly swim underwater to catch small fish, mollusks, and crustaceans. They usually swallow the food underwater.

But puffins bring food to their young in a different way. They carry the prey in their bills. An Atlantic puffin carrying several fish in its bill looks funny. It carries them crosswise. The heads and tails hang out of the bill's sides.

Puma
Puma concolor

Length: 3½ to 6½ feet
Weight: to 225 pounds
Diet: deer, sheep, antelope, rodents, rabbits and hares
Number of Young: 3 to 4

Home: North and South America
Order: carnivores
Family: cats

Forests and Mountains

Mammals

Endangered Animals

© CHARLES KREBS / CORBIS

Pumas once lived in most of the Western Hemisphere. Today, they live in a small part of this area. The only place they are found east of the Mississippi River is Florida. But just a few remain there. The Puma is one of the largest American cats. It has many names. It is also called cougar, mountain lion, panther, or catamount.

It has not always been very well liked. Pumas were known to kill cattle. So ranchers used to hunt and trap the large cats. Today, however, we realize that the puma actually helps ranchers and farmers. It eats deer, rodents, and other animals that eat the feed farmers give their animals.

Pumas are most active in the morning and at night. They hunt alone. Pumas are great climbers. They can leap as far as 20 feet. And they can run quickly. The puma stalks its prey and leaps on it. It kills it with a bite on the neck. A male can kill up to 100 small mammals a year. The puma stays in the same area for several years. It is able to live in tropical forests, pampas, and mountains. The males stay away from one another. They do not fight.

Pumas mate in all seasons. The female gives birth to three or four cubs every two years. They use the same den for several years at a time. The den is hidden between the rocks or in a thick covering of leaves and moss. The den is a shelter for the young. They are born with beautiful spotted fur.

Ball Python
Python regius

Length: 3 to 5 feet
Diet: small mammals and birds
Number of Eggs: about 100

Home: tropical West Africa
Order: scaled reptiles
Family: pythons

 Rain Forests

Reptiles

© JOE MCDONALD / ANIMALS ANIMALS / EARTH SCENES

The ball python is a constrictor. This means that it wraps itself around its prey and strangles it. It holds its prey tightly with its pointed teeth that tilt backward. Then it opens its mouth wide and easily swallows its prey, usually a small mammal or a bird.

The ball python has a highly developed sense of smell, which it uses when hunting. It has a heat-sensitive organ between its eyes and nostrils that can detect even tiny changes in the air temperature. Animals give off body heat, so a rise in air temperature may indicate that an animal is near.

The ball python is more or less peaceful. It never attacks humans and poses no danger to them. So what does it so when it feels threatened and cannot escape? It rolls itself into a ball with its head in the middle.

The ball python lives in the wet forests and scrublands of West Africa. It often stretches out on a branch. It is a land animal. But it is also a good swimmer. Like boa constrictors, ball pythons have remnants of hind legs in the shape of two small spurs. The female ball python lays about 100 eggs and stays with them, unlike most reptiles. She curls herself around the eggs and lays her head on top of them. Although all snakes are cold-blooded, her body is slightly warmer than the air. During this time she eats very little and leaves the eggs only to drink. She remains in this position until the little pythons hatch two to three months later.

Common Quail
Coturnix coturnix

Length: 7 inches
Weight: 4 to 5 pounds
Diet: worms, pea plants, grains, and clover
Number of Eggs: 8 to 14

Home: Central Europe, Africa, Central Asia, and Japan
Order: pheasants, quails, and relatives
Family: grouse, partridges

 Cities, Towns, and Farms

 Birds

© CYRIL RUOSO / BIOS / PETER ARNOLD, INC.

The common quail used to be much more common. According to the Bible, gigantic flocks of these low-flying birds swooped across the Mediterranean Sea each fall. They were on their way to spend the winter in the Sinai Desert. During the summer, this quail thickly populated the steppes of Central Europe. Swarms of quail rose up from the fields in the evening and flew low over the ground. They filled the night with the gentle sound of their beating wings.

But these huge flocks have not been seen since the beginning of the century. The common quail is now rare in Central Europe. The excessive use of farm chemicals is to blame. Herbicides killed the weeds that the quail needed for food. And pesticides meant to destroy insects killed many birds as well.

Coturnix coturnix japonica is one subspecies of the common quail. It is still quite common as a domesticated bird. Its attractive and tasty eggs are considered a gourmet delicacy around the world. Originally, however, the Japanese kept this bird simply for pleasure. They loved the male cock's melodious call, which sounds like "pick wer-wick." The cock uses this call to scare off other males and to attract females. When he finds a hen, the cock offers her a token of his love. This is usually a small piece of food, which he holds in his beak. He then struts around his new mate with his feathers puffed out. He thus hopes to impress her with his beauty.

Raccoon
Procyon lotor

Length: 16 to 24 inches
Weight: 4½ to 26 pounds
Diet: small animals, seeds, and fruits
Number of Young: 3 to 4

Home: North and Central America
Order: carnivores
Family: coatis, raccoons, and relatives

 Forests and Mountains

 Mammals

© D. ROBERT & LORRI FRANZ / CORBIS

You can easily spot a raccoon. It has a black "bandit" mask on its pointed nose. And it has black rings on its tail. The raccoon is very common in North America. Raccoons hold food with their hands before putting it in their mouths. They eat mostly crayfish, frogs, and fish. They also eat seeds, berries, and dry fruits.

The raccoon comes out at night. It lives in the woods and bushy areas near watering holes. It makes its den in many places. It may make its home in a hollow tree. Or it could live in a split in a rock. It could even use a burrow abandoned by another animal. It does not truly hibernate. The raccoon falls into a light sleep in the winter. It occasionally wakes up and goes outside. It loses almost half of its weight at this time.

Mating takes place in the spring. The young are born two months later. A litter has three to four young. The young weigh about 2½ ounces each. Newborn raccoons open their eyes at three months. They soon leave their burrow, with their mother watching over them.

An adult male lives in a territory about 100 acres in size. One to three females and several young live in the same territory. The raccoon does not defend its territory. It leads a solitary life. It avoids its own kind as much as possible. In the suburbs, raccoons often raid gardens and garbage pails. In the countryside, they damage crops such as melons and sweet corn.

Prairie Rattlesnake
Crotalus viridis

Length: 15 to 65 inches;
   typically 35 to 45 inches
Diet: rodents, birds, and other
   small vertebrates
Number of Young: 5 to 25

Home: central and western
   North America
Order: scaled reptiles
Family: pit vipers, vipers

  Grasslands

Reptiles

© W. PERRY CONWAY / CORBIS

Like all rattlesnakes, the prairie rattlesnake has a "sixth sense"—a built-in heat sensor! A small pit located in the rattler's head can sense warmth. When a warm-blooded animal comes near, nerve endings in the pit detect heat given off by the prey. They allow the rattler to know the victim is there even if the snake cannot see it. This sixth sense is extremely useful. It allows the snake to hunt in dark underground burrows and at night. The prairie rattlesnake can land a deadly bite without even seeing its victim.

Prairie rattlesnakes are quite common in prairies, forests, and coastal sand dunes covered with shrubs. They are also found on mountains, up to an elevation of about 8,000 feet. This snake usually lives alone. If

it lives in an area with cold winters, however, it will hibernate with others of its kind during the cold weather. Sometimes hundreds of rattlers will gather in a cave, burrow, or other den. Their bodies curl around one another, forming a solid ball of warmth.

At the end of the prairie rattlesnake's tail is a group of horny segments (called the rattle). It is from these that the creature gets its name. By vibrating these segments rapidly, the snake warns other animals to keep away. If an animal disregards this warning, the snake will strike. The rattlesnake sinks its sharp fangs into its prey, and poison flows through the fangs and into the victim's body. The poison may be powerful enough to kill a human!

Timber Rattlesnake
Crotalus horridus

Length: 3 to 6 feet
Diet: small birds and rodents
Number of Young: 5 to 17

Home: eastern United States
Order: scaled reptiles
Family: pit vipers, vipers

  Forests and Mountains

 Reptiles

© MARY ANN MCDONALD / CORBIS

The timber rattlesnake spends most of its waking hours coiled up and waiting in ambush. Motionless and beautifully camouflaged, the snake is nearly impossible to see in the underbrush. When a chipmunk, mouse, squirrel, or bird hops too near, the rattlesnake strikes with amazing speed. The venom in its hollow fangs is a deadly brew of chemicals that destroys the victim's blood. Unfortunately, the timber rattlesnake also remains motionless when humans approach. Before it is accidentally stepped on, the snake strikes, sometimes several times. The timber rattler's bite is very dangerous and requires immediate medical attention.

During cool weather, the snakes are most active during the day. But in midsummer, they avoid the heat by hunting at night. Timber rattlers mate in autumn, but females give birth only every other year, usually in September. As winter approaches, the snakes gather to hibernate in large numbers. They may nest among rocks or in abandoned animal dens.

Timber rattlers can be found in different colors, depending on their region. Those in the Northeast range from yellowish to brown, black, or gray. Those in the South may be pinkish gray or brown with tan or reddish stripes. All have dark blotches and broad bands of various colors.

Western Diamondback Rattlesnake
Crotalus atrox

Length: 3 to 7 feet
Weight: 13 pounds
Diet: small mammals, rodents, and birds
Number of Young: 10 to 20

Home: United States and Mexico
Order: scaled reptiles
Family: pit vipers, vipers

 Deserts

 Reptiles

© STEPHEN DALTON / PHOTO RESEARCHERS

Western diamondback rattlesnakes live in the United States. They are found from Missouri to California. They also dwell in northern Mexico. They live in all environments. They can make their homes in deserts, prairies, bush, woods, or river valleys. They are among the largest rattlers in the world. Rattlers are very dangerous. Their bites are deadly.

The famous "rattle" is found at the end of the tail. It is made up of scales shaped like rings. The rings are fitted one inside the other. They form a loose chain. The snake uses its tail when it feels threatened. It lifts its tail up and shakes the rattle hard. The rings vibrate and make a loud noise. It can be heard from more than 100 feet away. The more the snake feels threatened, the more it shakes its rattle.

Rattlesnakes are pit vipers. Pit vipers are a group of poisonous snakes. They are found in many parts of the world. They have a small dimple, or pit, between their eyes and nostrils. The pit can feel the smallest change in temperature. This "sixth sense" is very useful to the rattlesnake. It helps the snake spot its prey. The snake can even find its victims in the dark! The rattlesnake kills its prey with its two long poison fangs. About 20 people die in the United States each year from rattlesnake bites.

The Western diamondback rattlesnake gives birth to live young. Its eggs develop and hatch inside the female's body. The young are born in summer. There are usually 10 to 20 offspring.

Common Raven

Corvus corax

Length: 22 to 27 inches
Diet: carrion, small animals, bird eggs, nestlings, insects, garbage, and seeds
Number of Eggs: 4 to 6

Home: North America, Eurasia, and northern Africa
Order: perching birds
Family: crows, jays

 Forests and Mountains

 Birds

© JOE MCDONALD / CORBIS

The common raven is the largest of the world's perching birds. Along with its small cousin, the crow, the raven is among the most intelligent of birds. Breeding pairs generally mate for life, or at least for a very long time. During mating season, they are very affectionate, tapping their bills together and preening each other's feathers. Raven pairs soar high in the air with their wing tips touching. The male, in particular, is quite an acrobat. He seems to enjoy wheeling and tumbling in the air for no particular reason at all.

Ravens nest high in the trees, sometimes as much as 100 feet above the ground. They also build nests on tall buildings. A raven nest is a sturdy structure, woven out of branches, fat twigs, and shreds of bark. Year after year a mated pair may return to the same nest, repairing it as needed. Oddly enough, ravens never pick up sticks or other building materials that fall from their nest. As a result, the ground below is often covered with litter.

At one time the common raven was trapped and shot mercilessly. People believed it killed farm animals and wild game. Although ravens are often seen picking at the carcasses of large animals, the birds are only scavenging what another animal has killed. However, they do steal young chicks and break open unguarded eggs.

Darwin's Rhea
Pterocnemia pennata

Height: 5 feet
Weight: 60 pounds
Diet: vegetables, snails, lizards, and worms
Number of Eggs: 10 to 15

Home: Peru, Bolivia, Chile, and Argentina
Order: cassowaires, emus, and relatives
Family: rheas

 Grasslands

 Birds

© WOLFGANG KAEHLER / CORBIS

(?) Endangered Animals

The flightless rheas of South America look like the African ostrich. But they are only distant relatives. Darwin's rhea is named after the famous English naturalist Charles Darwin. It is the smaller of the two rhea species. It is found on the grassy eastern slopes of the dry Andes mountains.

Like ostriches, rheas make up for their lack of flight with long, powerful running legs. They can take steps of more than a yard each. Rheas would also be great in a game of dodgeball. When pursued by a predator, a speeding rhea can suddenly change direction with a violent flurry of its heavy wings.

For most of the year, the rhea lives in mixed groups of 10 to 30 birds. This changes in the spring, which is September through December in South America. At that time the adult males in a flock begin to fight. Eventually a single, dominant cock expels all other males. He is left alone with his hens.

The rhea cock is a very nontraditional father. He builds a single nest for all his "wives." They tend to be very careless about where they lay their eggs. The cock must follow after the hens, rolling their eggs back to his nest. Every hen in the flock lays 10 to 15 eggs. A typical male, however, is able to retrieve only 15 to 20. He incubates the eggs with no help from the females. He also cares for the chicks when they hatch.

Black Rhinoceros
Diceros bicornis

Length: 10 to 12 feet
Weight: 1½ tons
Diet: leaves of shrubs and grasses
Number of Young: 1

Home: sub-Saharan Africa
Order: odd-toed hoofed mammals
Family: rhinoceroses

 Grasslands

 Mammals

© JOE MCDONALD / CORBIS

? Endangered Animals

There are two kinds of rhinoceros—white and black. Actually, they both have a grayish skin. The only difference between the two is size, not color. This is how the confusion started. The rhinos live in East Africa. Dutch settlers there called the larger one "weit." This means "wide." English settlers thought this was "white."

The black rhinoceros lives in East Africa. It is found in the bushy savanna or around the rivers. It eats leaves, fruits, roots, and shoots. It takes a daily mud bath. It does this in black marshy places. So, even though it is gray, it comes out of the mud bath looking black. This probably helped it get its name. The males live alone in a marked territory. They always take the same path to go from the pasture to drink water. That's how they make trails, even in thick bushes. The same trails are used by several males. They mark them with their urine. And they always leave their droppings in the same place.

Black rhinos reproduce at any time during the year. Births usually happen every two or three years. The newborn weighs about 90 pounds. It is weaned only after two years. The young rhinoceros reaches adult height by the age of seven. The black rhinoceros is nearsighted. It cannot see things far away. However, its senses of hearing and smell are well developed. It is a heavy animal. But it can charge very fast. And it can be dangerous if it is attacked or hurt.

Great Indian Rhinoceros
Rhinoceros unicornis

Length: about 11 feet
Height: 5½ to 6 feet
Weight: about 2 tons
Diet: mostly grasses; occasionally aquatic plants and tree twigs

Number of Young: 1
Home: northeastern India and Nepal
Order: odd-toed hoofed mammals
Family: rhinoceroses

  Grasslands

Mammals

Endangered
Animals

© JAMES WARWICH / NHPA / PHOTO RESEARCHERS

While other rhinos have two nose horns, the Indian rhinoceros has a single prong. So you can see why its species name is *unicornis*. The rhino uses its sharp horn and two long tusks to battle with predators as well as with other rhinos. The animal's thick skin is folded in a way that looks like plates of armor. But the hide is not tough enough to protect a rhino from another rhino's horn and tusks. Male Indian rhinos often gore each other to death when fighting over a bathing hole or a fertile female.

During the day, this rhinoceros likes to rest in muddy water. Park tourists visiting a bathing hole may see a cattle egret standing in the water in the middle of three gray spikes. The bird is actually standing on the submerged head of an Indian rhino, and the spikes are the rhino's horn and ears. Once every 60 seconds, the rhinoceros lifts it head out of the water to breathe. Bathing holes are important to the rhinoceros for two reasons. The water buoys the animal's body, providing a much-needed rest from carrying its tremendous weight. Also, the mud shields the rhino's skin from sunburn and protects it from biting insects.

The human population of India has crowded the great animals onto a few small patches of protected land. This makes survival difficult because the rhinos may need to travel great distances to escape flooding and drought.

Sumatran Rhinoceros
Dicerorhinus sumatrensis

Length of Body: 8 feet
Length of Tail: 20 inches
Weight: 1,600 pounds
Diet: twigs of bushes and small trees

Number of Young: 1
Home: Southeast Asia
Order: odd-toed hoofed mammals
Family: rhinoceroses

Rain Forests

Mammals

Endangered Animals

© MICHAEL DICK / ANIMALS ANIMALS / EARTH SCENES

Unlike other rhinos, the Sumatran rhinoceros has a fairly dense coat of hair. On its snout are two horns made of thousands of tiny strands of keratin. This is the same substance that makes up people's fingernails and the horns of cows. Unlike a cow's horn, a rhino's horn is completely solid. The rhino uses its horns as a weapon.

The Sumatran rhino lives along the edges of rain forests. There it can hide among dense vegetation and bathe in muddy rivers. The rhino relies on its excellent senses of smell and hearing to locate its food and family members.

Sumatran rhinos reproduce slowly. A female becomes pregnant only once every three years and gives birth to one baby at a time. A baby rhino is well developed at birth, weighing about 75 pounds. It can stand when it is only an hour old. The mother nurses her youngster until it is 18 months old.

At one time, Sumatran rhinos were much more numerous than they are today. People have destroyed many of the forests that were home to the rhinos, and they kill the creatures for their horns. The horns are ground into powder for medicines used by Asians. Today scientists believe that only about 700 Sumatran rhinos remain on Earth. The species is in great danger of becoming extinct.

White Rhinoceros
Ceratotherium simum

Length of Body: 12 feet
Length of Tail: 28 inches
Height: 6 feet
Weight: 2 tons
Diet: grass

Number of Young: 1
Home: Zaïre and South Africa
Order: odd-toed hoofed mammals
Family: rhinoceroses

 Grasslands

 Mammals

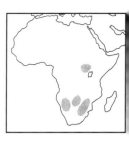

© W. PERRY CONWAY / CORBIS

Endangered Animals

A white rhino does not look very different from a black rhino. The two are similar in color. But they differ in size and shape. White rhinoceroses are larger and stockier than their cousins. The white rhinoceros is the second-largest land animal in the world. Only the elephant is larger.

The white rhino is also called the square-lipped rhinoceros. The black rhino has a pointed snout for eating bushes. But the white rhino has a flat snout. It is built for eating grass. The white rhino eats as it walks. It wraps its broad, leathery lips around clumps of grass. Then it sways its head from side to side. In this way, it rips up a big piece of grass wherever it goes. The white rhino has short legs and a long, curved skull. So this tank-sized lawn mower does not even have to bend its neck to reach the grass!

Humans are the only enemy of the rhinoceros. White rhinos almost became extinct in the 19th century. Big-game hunters killed almost all of them. Since then the government of South Africa has protected the species. More than 4,000 white rhinos live there today. But it is still endangered in other countries. It is illegal to kill any rhinoceros. Yet poachers still hunt them. They want the rhino's horns. The horns are very valuable. Some people believe that the horns have magical powers. This myth could spell doom for the white rhinoceros.

Greater Roadrunner
Geococcyx californianus

Length: 20 to 24 inches
Weight: 6 ounces
Diet: insects, reptiles, small rodents, small birds, and fruits

Number of Eggs: 3 to 6
Home: southwestern United States and Mexico
Order: cuckoos and relatives
Family: cuckoos

 Deserts

 Birds

© JOE MCDONALD / CORBIS

Roadrunners would rather race along the desert sand than fly in the air. They are just like the cartoon character that torments "Wile E. Coyote." They do fly, however, using their short wings for short trips. A roadrunner chasing an insect or lizard can reach speeds of 15 miles per hour.

According to cowboy legends, greater roadrunners are clever enough to outwit rattlesnakes. They will go out of their way to pick a fight. They can stab a snake to death with lightning-quick jabs. The roadrunner's amazing speed allows it to escape predators. It does this by scooting between rocks and cacti. It is also one of the few wild animals fast enough to dodge a speeding car. Most important, the bird's

agility enables it to pounce on the insects, lizards, mice, and small snakes. These are the animals that make up its diet. Early morning is the only time of day in which the roadrunner is not quick on its feet. This is because its body temperature drops considerably during the cold desert night. In the morning, it must bask in the sun until its temperature returns to normal.

Greater roadrunners mate for life. Together a mated pair will build a nest slightly off the ground. Favorite nesting places are low trees, shrubs, or cacti. The female roadrunner will lay three to six white or yellowish eggs. These hatch in about three weeks. Both parents share in the care of the newborn chicks.

American Robin
Turdus migratorius

Length: 10 inches
Diet: insects, worms, larvae, fruits, and berries
Number of Eggs: 3 to 6

Home: North America
Order: perching birds
Family: Old World flycatchers

  Cities, Towns, and Farms

Birds

© GARY W. CARTER / CORBIS

During the late winter, people in New England watch for a sure sign of spring. That sign is the red breast of the American robin. American robins live throughout North America. People wait for them where winters are cold and snowy.

Only the male robin has the striking red breast. The coloring of females is duller. Both sexes have a gray back and a long, thin yellow beak. And both have bold white markings around the eyes. Robins build a cup-shaped nest using grass and roots. These are held together with mud. A typical nest includes three to six eggs. The color of the eggs is so unusual it has its own name. It's called robin's egg blue. The eggs hatch in less than two weeks. Both parents care for the young. Robins often have two broods per season. When this happens, the male cares for the first brood. The female warms (incubates) the second.

The American robin can survive in many different places. It lives in woods, gardens, and city parks. It sings a clear, carol-like song. This bird flies south for the winter. It returns north in the spring. It is particularly fond of the worms it pulls from the ground. Robins also eat insects, larvae, and small invertebrates during the summer. In the winter and during bad weather their diet consists of fruits and berries.

A

aardvark **1**:5
acorn woodpecker **10**:37
Adelie penguin **7**:18
African bullfrog **2**:11
African elephant **3**:36
African wild ass **1**:18
Alabama water dog **10**:17
albatross, wandering **1**:6
alligator, American **1**:7
alpine ibex **5**:7
Amazon dolphin **3**:21
American alligator **1**:7
American anhinga **1**:10
American bison **1**:37
American bumblebee **2**:12
American cockroach **2**:37
American horsefly **4**:42
American lobster **5**:34
American marten **6**:6
American mink **6**:8
American robin **7**:44
American toad **9**:32
amphibians
    bullfrog **2**:10
    bullfrog, African **2**:11
    frog, Cuban tree **4**:13
    frog, green **4**:14
    frog, poison dart **4**:15
    frog, wood **4**:16
    peeper, spring **7**:17
    toad, American **9**:32
    toad, western spadefoot **9**:33
    water dog, Alabama **10**:17
anaconda, green **1**:8
Andean condor **2**:39
angelfish **1**:9
anhinga, American **1**:10
ant, army **1**:11
ant, black carpenter **1**:12
ant, fire **1**:13
anteater, giant **1**:14
ant-eating woodpecker (acorn
    woodpecker) **10**:37
Arabian camel **2**:16
Arabian oryx **6**:37
archerfish **1**:15
Arctic char **2**:24
Arctic fox **4**:9
Arctic ground squirrel **9**:8
Arctic tern **9**:25
armadillo, screaming hairy **1**:16
armadillo lizard **5**:31
army ant **1**:11
arthropods
    ant, army **1**:11
    ant, black carpenter **1**:12
    ant, fire **1**:13
    bed bug **1**:32
    bee, honey **1**:33
    beetle, Japanese **1**:34
    bumblebee, American **2**:12
    butterfly, monarch **2**:13
    caterpillar, woolly bear **2**:22
    centipede, house **2**:23
    cicada, seventeen-year **2**:30
    cockroach, American **2**:37
    crab, Florida stone **3**:6
    crab, giant hermit **3**:7
    crab, horseshoe **3**:8
    cricket, house **3**:11
    daddy longlegs (harvestman)
      3:14
    fiddler, Atlantic marsh **3**:41
    firefly, North American **3**:42
    fly, tsetse **4**:8
    fruit fly, common **4**:7
    horsefly, American **4**:42
    lobster, American **5**:34
    lobster, Caribbean spiny **5**:35
    mantis, praying **5**:44
    mosquito **6**:22
    moth, Atlas **6**:23
    moth, gypsy **6**:24
    moth, luna **6**:25
    nymph, common wood **6**:31
    shrimp, common **9**:32
    shrimp, northern pink **8**:33
    spider, black widow **8**:44
    spider, garden **9**:5

spider, house **9**:6
spider, wolf **9**:7
tarantula **9**:21
tarantula, desert blond **9**:22
termite, eastern subterranean
    9:24
water bug, giant **10**:16
weevil, boll **10**:19
yellow jacket, eastern **10**:42
Asian cobra **2**:34
Asian dhole **3**:18
Asian elephant **3**:37
Asiatic black bear **1**:28
asp **1**:17
ass, African wild **1**:18
Atlantic herring **4**:37
Atlantic marsh fiddler **3**:41
Atlantic puffin **7**:29
Atlantic razor clam **2**:31
Atlantic salmon **8**:6
Atlantic stingray **9**:13
Atlantic walrus **10**:12
Atlas moth **6**:23
aye-aye **1**:19

B

baboons
    chacma **1**:20
    gelada **1**:21
    hamadryas **1**:22
    yellow **1**:23
Bactrian camel **2**:17
badger, Eurasian **1**:24
bald eagle **3**:32
ball python **7**:31
banded linsang **5**:29
banded mongoose **6**:11
bandicoot, spiny **1**:25
Barbary macaque **5**:38
barn owl **6**:42
barn swallow **9**:15
barracuda, great **1**:26
bass, striped **1**:27
bay scallop **8**:12
bearded pig **7**:24
bearded seal **8**:18
bears
    Asiatic black **1**:28
    black **1**:29
    brown **1**:30
    panda, giant **7**:9
    panda, red **7**:10
    polar **1**:31
bed bug **1**:32
bee, honey **1**:33
beetle, Japanese **1**:34
beluga **1**:35
Bengal tiger **9**:28
bighorn sheep **8**:31
bird-eating spider (tarantula) **9**:21
bird of paradise, blue **1**:36
birds
    albatross, wandering **1**:6
    anhinga, American **1**:10
    blackbird, red-winged **1**:38
    bluebird, eastern **1**:39
    bluebird, mountain **1**:40
    blue bird of paradise **1**:36
    bobolink **2**:5
    booby, masked **2**:7
    booby, red-footed **2**:8
    bufflehead **2**:9
    buzzard, common **2**:14
    cardinal **2**:20
    cockatiel **2**:35
    cockatoo, sulphur-crested **2**:36
    condor, Andean **2**:39
    condor, California **2**:40
    crane, common **3**:9
    crane, whooping **3**:10
    dove, white-winged **3**:27
    duck, mandarin **3**:29
    duck, ruddy **3**:30
    duck, wood **3**:31
    eagle, bald **3**:32
    egret, snowy **3**:35
    falcon, peregrine **3**:38
    flamingo, greater **4**:6
    goose, Canada **4**:25
    goose, snow **4**:26
    grosbeak, evening **4**:28

grosbeak, rose-breasted **4**:29
gull, laughing **4**:31
heron, great blue **4**:35
heron, green-backed **4**:36
hornbill, great **4**:40
hornbill, rhinoceros **4**:41
hummingbird, broad-tailed
    4:43
hummingbird, ruby-throated
    4:44
ibis, scarlet **5**:8
jay, blue **5**:14
kingfisher **5**:18
kookaburra **5**:21
loon, common **5**:36
mallard **5**:40
meadowlark, eastern **6**:7
mockingbird **6**:9
nightingale **6**:30
oriole, golden **6**:36
osprey **6**:38
ostrich **6**:39
owl, barn **6**:42
owl, boreal **6**:43
owl, great horned **6**:44
owl, pygmy **7**:5
owl, screech **7**:6
owl, snowy **7**:7
parakeet, monk **7**:12
parrot, yellow-headed **7**:13
peafowl, Indian **7**:16
penguin, Adelie penguin **7**:18
penguin, chinstrap **7**:19
penguin, king **7**:20
penguin, little blue **7**:21
penguin, Magellanic **7**:22
pheasant, ring-necked **7**:23
pigeon, passenger **7**:25
pintail **7**:26
puffin, Atlantic **7**:29
quail, common **7**:32
raven, common **7**:37
rhea, Darwin's **7**:38
roadrunner, greater **7**:43
robin, American **7**:44
sandpiper, common **8**:10
sapsucker, yellow-bellied **8**:11
snipe, common **8**:42
sparrow, house **8**:43
starling, common **9**:12
swallow, barn **9**:15
swallow, cliff **9**:16
swan, black **9**:17
swan, trumpeter **9**:18
tern, Arctic **9**:25
tern, common **9**:26
titmouse, tufted **9**:31
toucan, toco **9**:36
turkey **9**:40
turkey, Latham's brush **9**:41
turtledove **10**:9
vulture, turkey **10**:11
warbler, Tennessee **10**:14
whippoorwill **10**:32
woodpecker, acorn **10**:37
woodpecker, ivory-billed
    10:38
woodpecker, red-headed **10**:39
wren, house **10**:40
bison, American **1**:37
black bear **1**:29
black bear, Asiatic **1**:28
blackbird, red-winged **1**:38
black carpenter ant **1**:12
black-footed ferret **3**:40
black howler monkey **6**:12
black rhinoceros **7**:39
black spider monkey **6**:13
black swan **9**:17
black widow spider **8**:44
blond tarantula, desert **9**:22
bluebird, eastern **1**:39
bluebird, mountain **1**:40
blue bird of paradise **1**:36
bluefin tuna **9**:39
bluefish **1**:41
blue heron, great **4**:35
blue jay **5**:14
blue limpet **5**:28
blue monkey **6**:14
blue shark **8**:24

blue skate **8**:35
blue whale **10**:20
boa, emerald tree **1**:43
boa constrictor **1**:42
bobcat **1**:44
bobolink **2**:5
boll weevil **10**:19
bonefish **2**:6
booby, masked **2**:7
booby, red-footed **2**:8
boreal owl **6**:43
bottle-nosed dolphin **3**:22
box turtle, common **9**:42
box turtle, ornate **10**:6
brain coral **2**:42
Brazilian tapir **9**:20
brindled gnu (wildebeest) **4**:23
broad-tailed hummingbird **4**:43
brown bear **1**:30
brown hyena **5**:5
brown lemur **5**:24
brush turkey, Latham's **9**:41
bufflehead **2**:9
bug, bed **1**:32
bullfrog **2**:10
bullfrog, African **2**:11
bumblebee, American **2**:12
Burgundy snail (edible snail)
    8:38
butterflies *see also* moths
    monarch **2**:13
    nymph, common wood **6**:31
buzzard, common **2**:14

C

caiman, dwarf **2**:15
California condor **2**:40
California moray **6**:21
California sea lion **8**:15
camel, Arabian **2**:16
camel, Bactrian **2**:17
Canada goose **4**:25
Canadian lynx **5**:37
Canadian otter **6**:40
cape pangolin **7**:11
capuchin, white-throated **2**:18
caracal **2**:19
cardinal **2**:20
Caribbean spiny lobster **5**:35
carpenter ant, black **1**:12
cat, sand **2**:21
catamount (puma) **7**:30
caterpillar, woolly bear **2**:22
cat shark, small-spotted **8**:28
centipede, house **2**:23
chacma baboon **1**:20
channeled whelk **10**:31
char, Arctic **2**:24
cheetah **2**:25
cheetah, king **2**:26
chimpanzee **2**:27
chimpanzee, pygmy **2**:28
chinchilla **2**:29
chinook salmon **8**:7
chinstrap penguin **7**:19
cicada, seventeen-year **2**:30
clam, Atlantic razor **2**:31
clam, giant **2**:32
clam, soft-shelled **2**:33
cliff swallow **9**:16
clown fish **3**:43
cobra, Asian **2**:34
cockatiel **2**:35
cockatoo, sulphur-crested **2**:36
cockroach, American **2**:37
Commerson's dolphin **3**:23
common, for names beginning
    see next part of name
conch, queen **2**:38
condor, Andean **2**:39
condor, California **2**:40
constrictor, boa **1**:42
copperhead **2**:41
coral, brain **2**:42
coral, large flower **2**:43
cottonmouth **2**:44
cougar (puma) **7**:30
coyote **3**:5
crabs
    Atlantic marsh fiddler **3**:41
    Florida stone **3**:6

crabs (cont.)
  giant hermit 3:7
  horseshoe 3:8
crane, common 3:9
crane, whooping 3:10
cricket, house 3:11
crocodile, Nile 3:12
crocodile, saltwater 3:13
Cuban tree frog 4:13

D

daddy longlegs (harvestman) 3:14
Darwin's rhea 7:38
De Brazza's monkey 6:16
deer, mule 3:15
deer, white-tailed 3:16
desert blond tarantula 9:22
desert iguana 5:9
desert lynx (caracal) 2:19
desert tortoise 9:34
devil, Tasmanian 3:17
dhole, Asian 3:18
diademed guenon (blue monkey)
  6:14
diamondback rattlesnake, western
  7:36
dingo 3:19
dogfish (small-spotted cat shark)
  8:28
dogs
  Asian dhole 3:18
  dingo 3:19
  raccoon dog 3:20
dolphin, Amazon 3:21
dolphin, bottle-nosed 3:22
dolphin, Commerson's 3:23
dolphin, common 3:24
dolphin, spotted 3:25
donkey 3:26
dove, turtle 10:9
dove, white-winged 3:27
drill 3:28
duck-billed platypus 7:27
duck hawk (peregrine falcon)
  3:38
ducks
  bufflehead 2:9
  mallard 5:40
  mandarin 3:29
  pintail 7:26
  ruddy 3:30
  wood 3:31
dwarf caiman 2:15

E

eagle, bald 3:32
earthworm (nightcrawler) 3:33
eastern bluebird 1:39
eastern gray squirrel 9:9
eastern grey kangaroo 5:16
eastern meadowlark 6:7
eastern oyster 7:8
eastern ribbon snake 8:40
eastern spotted skunk 8:36
eastern subterranean termite 9:24
eastern yellow jacket 10:42
edible sea urchin 8:17
edible snail 8:38
eel, electric 3:34
egret, great white (great blue
  heron) 4:35
egret, snowy 3:35
electric eel 3:34
elephant, African 3:36
elephant, Asian 3:37
elephant seal, northern 8:22
emerald tree boa 1:43
emperor tamarin 9:19
endangered animals
  ass, African wild 1:18
  aye-aye 1:19
  baboon, gelada 1:21
  bear, polar 1:31
  bobcat 1:44
  camel, Bactrian 2:17
  cat, sand 2:21
  cheetah 2:25
  cheetah, king 2:26
  chimpanzee, pygmy 2:28
  chinchilla 2:29

condor, Andean 2:39
condor, California 2:40
crab, horseshoe 3:8
crane, whooping 3:10
crocodile, saltwater 3:13
dhole, Asian 3:18
dingo 3:19
drill 3:28
eagle, bald 3:32
elephant, African 3:36
falcon, peregrine 3:38
ferret, black-footed 3:40
gibbon, hoolock 4:21
gorilla 4:27
hyena, brown 5:5
jaguar 5:13
lemur, brown 5:24
lemur, ring-tailed 5:25
leopard 5:26
leopard, snow 5:27
lynx, Canadian 5:37
macaque, liontail 5:39
marmoset, common 6:5
monkey, black howler 6:12
monkey, proboscis 6:18
ocelot 6:32
orangutan 6:35
oryx, Arabian 6:37
ostrich 6:39
otter, sea 6:41
panda, giant 7:9
panda, red 7:10
pangolin, cape 7:11
puma 7:30
rhea, Darwin's 7:38
rhinoceros, black 7:39
rhinoceros, great Indian 7:40
rhinoceros, Sumatran 7:41
rhinoceros, white 7:42
salmon, chinook 8:7
tapir, Brazilian 9:20
Tasmanian devil 3:17
tiger, Bengal 9:28
tiger, Siberian 9:29
tiger, Sumatra 9:30
tortoise, desert 9:34
tortoise, Galápagos 9:35
turtle, green sea 10:5
vicuña 10:10
vulture, turkey 10:11
whale, blue 10:20
whale, fin 10:22
whale, gray 10:23
whale, sperm 10:30
yak 10:41
ermine (long-tailed weasel) 10:18
estuarine crocodile (saltwater
  crocodile) 3:13
Eurasian badger 1:24
evening grosbeak 4:28
extinct animals
  pigeon, passenger 7:25
  wolf, Tasmanian 10:34
  woodpecker, ivory-billed
    10:38

F

fairy penguin (little blue penguin)
  7:21
falcon, peregrine 3:38
false killer whale 10:21
fennec 3:39
ferret, black-footed 3:40
fiddler, Atlantic marsh 3:41
fighting fish, Siamese 3:44
fin whale 10:22
fire ant 1:13
firefly, North American 3:42
fish
  angelfish 1:9
  archerfish 1:15
  barracuda, great 1:26
  bass, striped 1:27
  bluefish 2:7
  bonefish 2:6
  char, Arctic 2:24
  clown fish 3:43
  eel, electric 3:34
  gar, Florida 4:17
  goldfish 4:24
  guppy 4:32

herring, Atlantic 4:37
lamprey, sea 5:22
manta, giant 5:43
moray, California 6:21
parrotfish, queen 7:14
parrotfish, rainbow 7:15
porcupinefish 7:28
sailfin, giant 8:5
salmon, Atlantic 8:6
salmon, chinook 8:7
salmon, sockeye 8:8
sea horse, common 8:14
shark, blue 8:24
shark, great white 8:25
shark, nurse 8:26
shark, shortfin mako 8:27
shark, small-spotted cat 8:28
shark, tiger 8:29
shark, whale 8:30
Siamese fighting fish 3:44
skate, blue 8:35
snapper, red 8:41
stingray, Atlantic 9:13
sunfish, ocean 9:14
tarpon 9:23
tetra, flame 9:27
trout, lake 9:37
trout, rainbow 9:38
tuna, bluefin 9:39
zebrafish 10:44
fisher 4:5
flame tetra 9:27
flamingo, greater 4:6
Florida gar 4:17
Florida stone crab 3:6
flower coral, large 2:43
fly, common fruit 4:7
fly, tsetse 4:8
flying squirrel, southern 9:11
fox, Arctic 4:9
fox, gray 4:10
fox, kit 4:11
fox, red 4:12
frogs see also toads
  bullfrog 2:10
  bullfrog, African 2:11
  Cuban tree 4:13
  green 4:14
  peeper, spring 7:17
  poison dart 4:15
  wood 4:16
fruit fly, common 4:7
fur seal, northern 8:23

G

Galápagos tortoise 9:35
gar, Florida 4:17
garden spider 9:5
garter snake, common 8:39
gazelle, Thomson's 4:18
gecko, Moorish wall 4:19
gelada baboon 1:21
gerbil 4:20
giant anteater 1:14
giant clam 2:32
giant hermit crab 3:7
giant manta 5:43
giant Pacific octopus 6:34
giant panda 7:9
giant sailfin 8:5
giant water bug 10:16
gibbon, hoolock 4:21
giraffe 4:22
gnu, brindled (wildebeest) 4:23
golden dog (Asian dhole) 3:18
golden jackal 5:12
golden oriole 6:36
goldfish 4:24
goose, Canada 4:25
goose, snow 4:26
gorilla 4:27
gray fox 4:10
gray seal 8:19
gray squirrel, eastern 9:9
gray whale 10:23
gray wolf 10:33
great barracuda 1:26
great blue heron 4:35
greater flamingo 4:6
greater roadrunner 7:43
great hornbill 4:40

great horned owl 6:44
great Indian rhinoceros 7:40
great white egret (great blue
  heron) 4:35
great white shark 8:25
green anaconda 1:8
green-backed heron 4:36
green frog 4:14
green iguana 5:10
green mamba 5:41
green sea turtle 10:5
grey, kangaroo eastern 5:16
grizzly bear (brown bear) 1:30
grosbeak, evening 4:28
grosbeak, rose-breasted 4:29
groundhog (woodchuck) 10:36
ground squirrel, Arctic 9:8
guenon, diademed (blue monkey)
  6:14
guinea pig 4:30
gull, laughing 4:31
guppy 4:32
gypsy moth 6:24

H

hairy armadillo, screaming 1:16
hamadryas baboon 1:22
hamster, common 4:33
harbor seal 8:20
hare, snowshoe 4:34
harp seal 8:21
harvestman (daddy longlegs) 3:14
hawk, duck (peregrine falcon)
  3:38
headfish (ocean sunfish) 9:14
hermit crab, giant 3:7
heron, great blue 4:35
heron, green-backed 4:36
herring, Atlantic 4:37
hippopotamus 4:38
hippopotamus, pygmy 4:39
honey bee 1:33
hoolock gibbon 4:21
hornbill, great 4:40
hornbill, rhinoceros 4:41
horned owl, great 6:44
horsefly, American 4:42
horseshoe crab 3:8
house centipede 2:23
house cricket 3:11
house mouse 6:26
house sparrow 8:43
house spider 9:6
house wren 10:40
howler monkey, black 6:12
hummingbird, broad-tailed 4:43
hummingbird, ruby-throated 4:44
humpback whale 10:24
hyena, brown 5:5
hyena, laughing 5:6

I

ibex, alpine 5:7
ibis, scarlet 5:8
iguana, desert 5:9
iguana, green 5:10
impala 5:11
Indian peafowl 7:16
Indian rhinoceros, great 7:40
Indo-Pacific crocodile (saltwater
  crocodile) 3:13
invertebrates, other
  clam, Atlantic razor 2:31
  clam, giant 2:32
  clam, soft-shelled 2:33
  conch, queen 2:38
  coral, brain 2:42
  coral, large flower 2:43
  earthworm (nightcrawler) 3:33
  jellyfish, moon 5:15
  leech, medicinal 5:23
  limpet, blue 5:28
  man-of-war, Portuguese 5:42
  mussel, zebra 6:29
  octopus, common 6:33
  octopus, giant Pacific 6:34
  oyster, eastern 7:8
  sand dollar, common 8:9
  scallop, bay 8:12
  sea fan 8:13

sea star, common **8**:16
sea urchin, edible **8**:17
snail, edible **8**:38
whelk, channeled **10**:31
Isabella tiger moth (woolly bear caterpillar) **2**:22
ivory-billed woodpecker **10**:38

J-K

jackal, golden **5**:12
jaguar **5**:13
Japanese beetle **1**:34
jay, blue **5**:14
jellyfish, moon **5**:15
jungle dog (Asian dhole) **3**:18
kangaroo, eastern grey **5**:16
kangaroo, red **5**:17
killer whale **10**:25
killer whale, false **10**:21
king cheetah **2**:26
kingfisher **5**:18
king penguin **7**:20
king salmon (chinook salmon) **8**:7
kingsnake, common **5**:19
kit fox **4**:11
koala **5**:20
Kodiak bear (brown bear) **1**:30
kookaburra **5**:21

L

lake trout **9**:37
lamprey, sea **5**:22
large flower coral **2**:43
Latham's brush turkey **9**:41
laughing gull **4**:31
laughing hyena **5**:6
leech, medicinal **5**:23
lemur, brown **5**:24
lemur, ring-tailed **5**:25
leopard **5**:26
leopard, snow **5**:27
lightning bugs (fireflies) **3**:42
limpet, blue **5**:28
linsang, banded **5**:29
lion **5**:30
liontail macaque **5**:39
little blue penguin (fairy penguin) **7**:21
lizard, armadillo **5**:31
lizard, ornate tree **5**:32
llama **5**:33
lobster, American **5**:34
lobster, Caribbean spiny **5**:35
long-eared (screech owl) **7**:6
long-finned pilot whale **10**:26
long-tailed weasel **10**:18
loon, common **5**:36
luna moth **6**:25
lynx, Canadian **5**:37
lynx, desert (caracal) **2**:19

M

macaque, Barbary **5**:38
Magellanic penguin **7**:22
mako shark, shortfin **8**:27
mallard **5**:40
mamba, green **5**:41
mammals
    aardvark **1**:5
    anteater, giant **1**:14
    armadillo, screaming hairy **1**:16
    ass, African wild **1**:18
    aye-aye **1**:19
    baboon, chacma **1**:20
    baboon, gelada **1**:21
    baboon, hamadryas **1**:22
    baboon, yellow **1**:23
    badger, Eurasian **1**:24
    bandicoot, spiny **1**:25
    bear, Asiatic black **1**:28
    bear, black **1**:29
    bear, brown **1**:30
    bear, polar **1**:31
    beluga **1**:35
    bison, American **1**:37
    bobcat **1**:44
    camel, Arabian **2**:16
    camel, Bactrian **2**:17

capuchin, white-throated **2**:18
caracal **2**:19
cat, sand **2**:21
cheetah **2**:25
cheetah, king **2**:26
chimpanzee **2**:27
chimpanzee, pygmy **2**:28
chinchilla **2**:29
coyote **3**:5
deer, mule **3**:15
deer, white-tailed **3**:16
dhole, Asian **3**:18
dingo **3**:19
dog, raccoon **3**:20
dolphin, Amazon **3**:21
dolphin, bottle-nosed **3**:22
dolphin, Commerson's **3**:23
dolphin, common **3**:24
dolphin, spotted **3**:25
donkey **3**:26
drill **3**:28
elephant, African **3**:36
elephant, Asian **3**:37
fennec **3**:39
ferret, black-footed **3**:40
fisher **4**:5
fox, Arctic **4**:9
fox, gray **4**:10
fox, kit **4**:11
fox, red **4**:12
gazelle, Thomson's **4**:18
gerbil **4**:20
gibbon, hoolock **4**:21
giraffe **4**:22
gnu, brindled (wildebeest) **4**:23
gorilla **4**:27
guinea pig **4**:30
hamster, common **4**:33
hare, snowshoe **4**:34
hippopotamus **4**:38
hippopotamus, pygmy **4**:39
hyena, brown **5**:5
hyena, laughing **5**:6
ibex, alpine **5**:7
impala **5**:11
jackal, golden **5**:12
jaguar **5**:13
kangaroo, eastern grey **5**:16
kangaroo, red **5**:17
koala **5**:20
lemur, brown **5**:24
lemur, ring-tailed **5**:25
leopard **5**:26
leopard, snow **5**:27
linsang, banded **5**:29
lion **5**:30
llama **5**:33
lynx, Canadian **5**:37
macaque, Barbary **5**:38
macaque, liontail **5**:39
marmoset, common **6**:5
marten, American **6**:6
mink, American **6**:8
mole, star-nosed **6**:10
mongoose, banded **6**:11
monkey, black howler **6**:12
monkey, black spider **6**:13
monkey, blue **6**:14
monkey, common squirrel **6**:15
monkey, De Brazza's **6**:16
monkey, night **6**:17
monkey, proboscis **6**:18
monkey, rhesus **6**:19
moose **6**:20
mouse, house **6**:26
muskox **6**:27
muskrat **6**:28
ocelot **6**:32
orangutan **6**:35
oryx, Arabian **6**:37
otter, Canadian **6**:40
otter, sea **6**:41
panda, giant **7**:9
panda, red **7**:10
pangolin, cape **7**:11
pig, bearded **7**:24
platypus, duck-billed **7**:27
puma **7**:30
raccoon **7**:33

rhinoceros, black **7**:39
rhinoceros, great Indian **7**:40
rhinoceros, Sumatran **7**:41
rhinoceros, white **7**:42
seal, bearded **8**:18
seal, gray **8**:19
seal, harbor **8**:20
seal, harp **8**:21
seal, northern elephant **8**:22
seal, northern fur **8**:23
sea lion, California **8**:15
sheep, bighorn **8**:31
skunk, eastern spotted **8**:36
squirrel, Arctic ground **9**:8
squirrel, eastern gray **9**:9
squirrel, red **9**:10
squirrel, southern flying **9**:11
tamarin, emperor **9**:19
tapir, Brazilian **9**:20
Tasmanian devil **3**:17
tiger, Bengal **9**:28
tiger, Siberian **9**:29
tiger, Sumatra **9**:30
vicuña **10**:10
walrus, Atlantic **10**:12
walrus, Pacific **10**:13
warthog **10**:15
weasel, long-tailed **10**:18
whale, blue **10**:20
whale, false killer **10**:21
whale, fin **10**:22
whale, gray **10**:23
whale, humpback **10**:24
whale, killer **10**:25
whale, long-finned pilot **10**:26
whale, Pacific pilot **10**:27
whale, pygmy right **10**:28
whale, pygmy sperm **10**:29
whale, sperm **10**:30
wolf, gray **10**:33
wolf, Tasmanian **10**:34
wombat, common **10**:35
woodchuck **10**:36
yak **10**:41
zebra, plains **10**:43
mandarin duck **3**:29
man-of-war, Portuguese **5**:42
manta, giant **5**:43
mantis, praying **5**:44
marmoset, common **6**:5
marsupials
    bandicoot, spiny **1**:25
    common wombat **10**:35
    eastern grey kangaroo **5**:16
    koala **5**:20
    red kangaroo **5**:17
    Tasmanian devil **3**:17
    Tasmanian wolf **10**:34
marten, American **6**:6
masked booby **2**:7
meadowlark, eastern **6**:7
medicinal leech **5**:23
mink, American **6**:8
mockingbird **6**:9
mola (ocean sunfish) **9**:14
mole, star-nosed **6**:10
monarch butterfly **2**:13
mongoose, banded **6**:11
monkeys see also baboons
    black howler **6**:12
    black spider **6**:13
    blue **6**:14
    capuchin, white-throated **2**:18
    common squirrel **6**:15
    De Brazza's **6**:16
    macaque, Barbary **5**:38
    macaque, liontail **5**:39
    marmoset, common **6**:5
    night **6**:17
    proboscis **6**:18
    rhesus **6**:19
monk parakeet **7**:12
moon bear (Asiatic black bear) **1**:28
moonfish (ocean sunfish) **9**:14
moon jellyfish **5**:15
Moorish wall gecko **4**:19
moose **6**:20
moray, California **6**:21
mosquito **6**:22

moths see also butterflies
    Atlas **6**:23
    gypsy **6**:24
    Isabella tiger (woolly bear) **2**:22
    luna **6**:25
mountain bluebird **1**:40
mountain lion (puma) **7**:30
mouse, house **6**:26
mud turtle, common **9**:43
mule deer **3**:15
muskox **6**:27
muskrat **6**:28
musk turtle, common **9**:44
mussel, zebra **6**:29

N

nightcrawler (earthworm) **3**:33
nightingale **6**:30
night monkey **6**:17
Nile crocodile **3**:12
North American firefly **3**:42
northern elephant seal **8**:22
northern fur seal **8**:23
northern pink shrimp **8**:33
nurse shark **8**:26
nymph, common wood **6**:31

O

ocean sunfish **9**:14
octopus, common **6**:33
octopus, giant Pacific **6**:34
orangutan **6**:35
oriole, golden **6**:36
ornate box turtle **10**:6
ornate tree lizard **5**:32
oryx, Arabian **6**:37
osprey **6**:38
ostrich **6**:39
otter, Canadian **6**:40
otter, sea **6**:41
owl, barn **6**:42
owl, boreal **6**:43
owl, great horned **6**:44
owl, pygmy **7**:5
owl, screech **7**:6
owl, snowy **7**:7
oyster, eastern **7**:8

P

Pacific octopus, giant **6**:34
Pacific pilot whale **10**:27
Pacific walrus **10**:13
painted turtle **10**:7
panda, giant **7**:9
panda, red **7**:10
pangolin, cape **7**:11
panther (puma) **7**:30
parakeet, monk **7**:12
parrot, yellow-headed **7**:13
parrotfish, queen **7**:14
parrotfish, rainbow **7**:15
passenger pigeon **7**:25
peafowl, Indian **7**:16
peeper, spring **7**:17
penguin, Adelie **7**:18
penguin, chinstrap **7**:19
penguin, king **7**:20
penguin, little blue **7**:21
penguin, Magellanic **7**:22
peregrine falcon **3**:38
pheasant, ring-necked **7**:23
pig, bearded **7**:24
pigeon, passenger **7**:25
pilot whale, long-finned **10**:26
pilot whale, Pacific **10**:27
pink shrimp, northern **8**:33
pintail **7**:26
plains zebra **10**:43
platypus, duck-billed **7**:27
poison dart frog **4**:15
polar bear **1**:31
porcupinefish **7**:28
Portuguese man-of war **5**:42
prairie rattlesnake **7**:34
praying mantis **5**:44
proboscis monkey **6**:18
puffin, Atlantic **7**:29
puma **7**:30

pygmy chimpanzee **2**:28
pygmy hippopotamus **4**:39
pygmy owl **7**:5
pygmy right whale **10**:28
pygmy sperm whale **10**:29
python, ball **7**:31

Q-R

quail, common **7**:32
queen conch **2**:38
queen parrotfish **7**:14
raccoon **7**:33
raccoon dog **3**:20
rainbow parrotfish **7**:15
rainbow trout **9**:38
rattlesnake, prairie **7**:34
rattlesnake, timber **7**:35
rattlesnake, western diamondback **7**:36
raven, common **7**:37
razor clam, Atlantic **2**:31
red-breasted baboon (gelada baboon) **1**:21
red dog (Asian dhole) **3**:18
red-footed booby **2**:8
red fox **4**:12
red-headed woodpecker **10**:39
red hermit crab (giant hermit crab) **3**:7
red kangaroo **5**:17
red panda **7**:10
red snapper **8**:41
red squirrel **9**:10
red-winged blackbird **1**:38
reptiles *see also* snakes
    alligator, American **1**:7
    caiman, dwarf **2**:15
    crocodile, Nile **3**:12
    crocodile, saltwater **3**:13
    gecko, Moorish wall **4**:19
    iguana, desert **5**:9
    iguana, green **5**:10
    lizard, armadillo **5**:31
    lizard, ornate tree **5**:32
    slider **8**:37
    tortoise, desert **9**:34
    tortoise, Galápagos **9**:35
    turtle, common box **9**:42
    turtle, common mud **9**:43
    turtle, common musk **9**:44
    turtle, green sea **10**:5
    turtle, ornate box **10**:6
    turtle, painted **10**:7
    turtle, snapping **10**:8
rhea, Darwin's **7**:38
rhesus monkey **6**:19
rhinoceros, black **7**:39
rhinoceros, great Indian **7**:40
rhinoceros, Sumatran **7**:41
rhinoceros, white **7**:42
rhinoceros hornbill **4**:41
ribbon snake, eastern **8**:40
right whale, pygmy **10**:28
ring-necked pheasant **7**:23
ring-tailed lemur **5**:25
roadrunner, greater **7**:43
robin, American **7**:44
rose-breasted grosbeak **4**:29
ruby-throated hummingbird **4**:44
ruddy duck **3**:30

S

sailfin, giant **8**:5
salmon, Atlantic **8**:6
salmon, chinook **8**:7
salmon, sockeye **8**:8
saltwater crocodile **3**:13
sand cat **2**:21
sand dollar, common **8**:9
sandpiper, common **8**:10
sapsucker, yellow-bellied **8**:11

scallop, bay **8**:12
scarlet ibis **5**:8
screaming hairy armadillo **1**:16
screech owl **7**:6
sea cake (common sand dollar) **8**:9
sea fan **8**:13
sea horse, common **8**:14
seal, bearded **8**:18
seal, gray **8**:19
seal, harbor **8**:20
seal, harp **8**:21
seal, northern elephant **8**:22
seal, northern fur **8**:23
sea lamprey **5**:22
sea lion, California **8**:15
sea otter **6**:41
sea star, common **8**:16
sea turtle, green **10**:5
sea urchin, edible **8**:17
seventeen-year cicada **2**:30
shark, blue **8**:24
shark, great white **8**:25
shark, nurse **8**:26
shark, shortfin mako **8**:27
shark, small-spotted cat **8**:28
shark, tiger **8**:29
shark, whale **8**:30
sheep, bighorn **8**:31
shivering owl (screech owl) **7**:6
shortfin mako shark **8**:27
shrimp, common **8**:32
shrimp, northern pink **8**:33
Siamese fighting fish **3**:44
Siberian tiger **9**:29
Siberian wild dog (Asian dhole) **3**:18
sidewinder **8**:34
skate, blue **8**:35
skunk, eastern spotted **8**:36
slender-beaked dolphin (spotted dolphin) **3**:25
slider **8**:37
small-spotted cat shark **8**:28
snail, edible **8**:38
snakebird (American anhinga) **1**:10
snakes
    anaconda, green **1**:8
    asp **1**:17
    boa, emerald tree **1**:43
    boa constrictor **1**:42
    cobra, Asian **2**:34
    copperhead **2**:41
    cottonmouth **2**:44
    garter snake, common **8**:39
    kingsnake, common **5**:19
    mamba, green **5**:41
    python, ball **7**:31
    rattlesnake, prairie **7**:34
    rattlesnake, timber **7**:35
    rattlesnake, western diamondback **7**:36
    ribbon snake, eastern **8**:40
    sidewinder **8**:34
snapper, red **8**:41
snapping turtle **10**:8
snipe, common **8**:42
snow goose **4**:26
snow leopard **5**:27
snowshoe hare **4**:34
snowy egret **3**:35
snowy owl **7**:7
sockeye salmon **8**:8
soft-shelled clam **2**:33
southern flying squirrel **9**:11
spadefoot toad, western **9**:33
sparrow, house **8**:43
sperm whale **10**:30
sperm whale, pygmy **10**:29
spider monkey, black **6**:13

spiders
    black widow **8**:44
    garden **9**:5
    house **9**:6
    tarantula **9**:21
    tarantula, desert blond **9**:22
    wolf **9**:7
spiny bandicoot **1**:25
spiny lobster, Caribbean **5**:35
spotted dolphin **3**:25
spotted skunk, eastern **8**:36
spring peeper **7**:17
square-lipped rhinoceros (white rhinoceros) **7**:42
squirrel, Arctic ground **9**:8
squirrel, eastern gray **9**:9
squirrel, red **9**:10
squirrel, southern flying **9**:11
squirrel monkey, common **6**:15
starfish (sea star) **8**:16
starling, common **9**:12
star-nosed mole **6**:10
steelhead trout (rainbow trout) **9**:38
stingray, Atlantic **9**:13
stone crab, Florida **3**:6
striped bass **1**:27
subterranean termite, eastern **9**:24
sulphur-crested cockatoo **2**:36
Sumatran rhinoceros **7**:41
Sumatra tiger **9**:30
sunfish, ocean **9**:14
swallow, barn **9**:15
swallow, cliff **9**:16
swan, black **9**:17
swan, trumpeter **9**:18

T

tamarin, emperor **9**:19
tapir, Brazilian **9**:20
tarantula **9**:21
tarantula, desert blond **9**:22
tarpon **9**:23
Tasmanian devil **3**:17
Tasmanian wolf **10**:34
Tengmalm's owl (boreal owl) **6**:43
Tennessee warbler **10**:14
termite, eastern subterranean **9**:24
tern, Arctic **9**:25
tern, common **9**:26
tetra, flame **9**:27
Thomson's gazelle **4**:18
tiger, Bengal **9**:28
tiger, Siberian **9**:29
tiger, Sumatra **9**:30
tiger moth, Isabella (woolly bear caterpillar) **2**:22
tiger shark **8**:29
timber rattlesnake **7**:35
titmouse, tufted **9**:31
toads *see also* frogs
    American **9**:32
    western spadefoot **9**:33
toco toucan **9**:36
tortoises *see also* turtles
    desert **9**:34
    Galápagos **9**:35
toucan, toco **9**:36
tree boa, emerald **1**:43
tree fox (gray fox) **4**:10
tree frog, Cuban **4**:13
tree lizard, ornate **5**:32
trout, lake **9**:37
trout, rainbow **9**:38
trumpeter swan **9**:18
tsetse fly **4**:8
tufted titmouse **9**:31
tuna, bluefin **9**:39
turkey **9**:40
turkey, Latham's brush **9**:41

turkey vulture **10**:11
turtledove **10**:9
turtles *see also* tortoises
    common box **9**:42
    common mud **9**:43
    common musk **9**:44
    green sea **10**:5
    ornate box **10**:6
    painted **10**:7
    slider **8**:37
    snapping **10**:8

U-V-W

vicuña **10**:10
vulture, turkey **10**:11
wall gecko, Moorish **4**:19
walrus, Atlantic **10**:12
walrus, Pacific **10**:13
wandering albatross **1**:6
warbler, Tennessee **10**:14
warthog **10**:15
water bug, giant **10**:16
water bug (American cockroach) **2**:37
water dog, Alabama **10**:17
weasel, long-tailed **10**:18
weevil, boll **10**:19
western diamondback rattlesnake **7**:36
western spadefoot toad **9**:33
whales
    beluga **1**:35
    blue **10**:20
    false killer **10**:21
    fin **10**:22
    gray **10**:23
    humpback **10**:24
    killer **10**:25
    long-finned pilot **10**:26
    Pacific pilot **10**:27
    pygmy right **10**:28
    pygmy sperm **10**:29
    sperm **10**:30
whale shark **8**:30
whelk, channeled **10**:31
whippoorwill **10**:32
white egret, great (great blue heron) **4**:35
white oryx (Arabian oryx) **6**:37
white rhinoceros **7**:42
white shark, great **8**:25
white-tailed deer **3**:16
white-throated capuchin **2**:18
white whale (beluga) **1**:35
white-winged dove **3**:27
whooping crane **3**:10
wild ass, African **1**:18
wildebeest (brindled gnu) **4**:23
wolf, gray **10**:33
wolf, Tasmanian **10**:34
wolf spider **9**:7
wombat, common **10**:35
woodchuck **10**:36
wood duck **3**:31
wood frog **4**:16
wood nymph, common **6**:31
woodpecker, acorn **10**:37
woodpecker, ivory-billed **10**:38
woodpecker, red-headed **10**:39
woolly bear caterpillar **2**:22
wren, house **10**:40

X-Y-Z

yak **10**:41
yellow baboon **1**:23
yellow-bellied sapsucker **8**:11
yellow-headed parrot **7**:13
yellow jacket, eastern **10**:42
zebra, plains **10**:43
zebrafish **10**:44
zebra mussel **6**:29